Redford Township District Library
25320 West Six Mile Road
Redford, MI 48240

www.redford.lib.mi.us

Hours:

Mon-Thur 10-8:30
Fri-Sat   10-5
Sunday (School Year) 12-5

LIFE LESSONS FROM SOCCER

What Your Child Can Learn
on and off the Field—A Guide
for Parents and Coaches

Vincent Fortanasce, M.D.

A Fireside Book
Published by Simon & Schuster
New York   London   Toronto   Sydney   Singapore

FIRESIDE
Rockefeller Center
1230 Avenue of the Americas
New York, NY 10020

For information about special discounts for bulk purchases,
please contact Simon & Schuster Special Sales:
1-800-456-6798 or business@simonandschuster.com

Designed by William Ruoto

Manufactured in the United States of America

1 3 5 7 9 10 8 6 4 2

Library of Congress Cataloging-in-Publication Data

Fortanasce, Vincent.
Life lessons from soccer : what your child can learn on and off the field : a guide for
parents and coaches / Vincent Fortanasce.
p. cm.
"A Fireside book."
Includes index.
1. Soccer for children—Psychological aspects. I. Title.
GV944.2 .F67 2001
796.334—dc21   2001033630

ISBN 0-7432-0575-8

Acknowledgments

This book could not have come into being without the assistance of many people. First, I would like to thank my family: my children, Vinnie and Kaycee and Michael, who helped with the drawings; my siblings, Joan, Elaine, and Michael; my niece, Gerilyn, and nephew, Mark, and their children.

My friends supported me and shared their stories: Dino and Hope Clarizio, Don and Judy Norquist, Mary and Schuck, Nancy and Michael Iredale, Mel Apt, Ed Todd, Charlie Imbus, Rick Shubin, Ken Wogensen, Brent and Chris Miller, Richard and Mary Vanis, Charles Eastman, Karen Dardeck, Mike Habib, Dennis and Carolyn Lee, Melodie and Tammy Atkinson, and Neil Romano.

Special thanks to Lawrence Robinson and Doris Cooper, who helped with writing the manuscript, and to Amy Rennert, my agent. To Gayle Hartell for his psychological insights.

At the American Youth Soccer Organization I would like to thank Dick Wilson, Cathy Ferguson, Rise Reading, Mark Auch, and John Ouelette, national coach of AYSO.

I cannot thank you all enough for your support, love, and assistance.

To the woman who held me when I was a child, consoled me as an adolescent, encouraged me as a young man, and is my inspiration. Truly the saint of soccer, my mom, Rose Fortanasce.

Contents

Introduction

Soccer, like music and art, is one of those precious gifts that gives value to life.

Life Lessons from Soccer is about the complex relationships among parents, coaches, and children on the soccer field. Its focus is one of a child's first treks through life, one guided principally by parents. It's about the true goals of soccer: the development of perseverance, courage, and character. It is about changing parents' and coaches' concepts that a child is born a winner or a loser, intelligent or stupid, agile or awkward.

The great soccer player Pelé once said, "School is for the child. But soccer is for the family and child." The soccer field is the family's field of opportunity. It bestows an opportunity to learn the life lessons of:

1. Support
2. Friendship
3. Competition
4. Victory
5. Defeat
6. Care, courage, and character
7. The exceptional bond between parent and child and community

8. Presence, attitude, acceptance, and communication
9. Love

Life Lessons from Soccer includes true stories, some humorous, some sobering. The names used are fictitious and often used to illustrate the point and focus: Mr. Excuski, Mrs. Bigwig, Mr. Sherman, and Hank "the Horrible," to name a few. Sometimes I have combined scenarios, for the sake of being concise, but I hope that each story will enhance your understanding of your child and your unique relationship with him or her.

Experience gives you life's consequences, then teaches you the lesson. *Life Lessons from Soccer* is written so you can learn from the experiences of my life as a dad, coach, and physician.

1

Dreams

The 1st Life Lesson:
A Child Without a Dream Is Like a Boat Without a Sail

Seven-year-old Kathy beamed a smile that could have brightened the rainiest of days. "Mom, Mom!" she cried out excitedly. Her mother was pouring milk into a mug with a picture of Madonna on the side. "What is it?" she asked.

"I know what I want to be when I grow up! I want to be like Mia Hamm!"

Her mother sighed. "She's not another rock star, is she?"

"No, Mom, she's the greatest soccer player ever! I'm gonna be like her, you watch." Her words were spoken with the absolute certainty that only fantasy-laden children can muster. "Can I get a soccer ball and a poster of her maybe? I'll clean my room and vacuum forever. I promise, I promise."

Kathy's mom, a corporate lawyer, sighed again and, in the same tone a jury foreman might use to declare a defendant guilty, said, "No. Stop filling your head with childish dreams. You've never even played soccer before, how can you be the greatest player? Eat breakfast, finish your homework, and get ready for school." Suddenly a chill wind swept the sunshine from Kathy's face and clouds covered the twinkle in her eyes. "Don't you realize it's only study and hard work that will help you make something of your life? It's a degree you need, not a poster!"

With a few simple words, both Kathy and her dream had been crushed.

Dreams

Dreams are an inspiration to children. Yes, they are childhood dreams—to be a professional soccer player, a firefighter, a rock star, or an actress—but children see these people on TV and it's exciting to them. It's what they talk about at school. Most important, dreams provide motivation, purpose, and direction for a child, no matter how unlikely the dreams are. Nurture the dreams and they will bring spirit, determination, and pleasure to your child. After all, success ultimately is determined by the joy in life.

Those childhood dreams will change with age, just as eight-year-old boys hate girls and then grow to love them at eighteen.

Today's Dream May Be Tomorrow's Reality

Sam wanted to be a soccer player like the great Brazilian player Pelé. But Sam was the smallest in his class, slow, and not very skillful with a soccer ball.

However, his parents never wavered. They brought him to

every North American Soccer League game, especially when the New York Cosmos and Pelé were playing. They helped Sam pin a giant poster of Pelé on his bedroom wall and Sam worked hard to play as well as he could.

Ten years later, Sam's dream changed. He wanted to be a doctor. He went after that dream with the same zeal that he had pursued his dream of being a soccer player. He graduated medical school near the top of his class. His parents taught him as a child to follow his dream. They thought he could do whatever he set his mind to do. And, as a result, so did Sam.

Too many parents stamp out childhood dreams with adult realities. In doing so they stamp out a child's hope and motivation, they quash the sunshine and starry-eyed fantasies that make childhood so special.

We Don't Remember Days, Only Moments

I can still remember the moment one cloudy Saturday morning when my dad asked me to fetch the mower from the garage to cut the lawn. You might ask why this is such a memorable moment. Well, it was my tenth birthday and it appeared that my parents had forgotten. I dutifully trudged to the garage and pulled open the door. I moved some boxes and a bike out of the way and finally uncovered the mower. My parents stood behind me, staring in disbelief as I slowly pushed it out. My dad cleared his throat. "Hey, Vin." I looked up at him, feeling very sorry for myself. I couldn't believe they'd forgotten my birthday. He smiled at my mom, then patted me on the head. "How are you going to win the Tour de France?" I frowned, then followed his gaze over to the bike. It was a gleaming ten-speed racer. My birthday present! I hadn't even noticed it. In a flash I was a bundle of excitement, my head filled with images of winning the bicycle race of bicycle races, the Tour de France. I carried this dream with me for a long time. I never raced in the Tour, of course, only with the other kids on my block, but I still remember the moment my parents ignited my childhood dream. They believed in me.

 ## From the Doctor's Desk

Several studies have shown that parents who nurture childhood dreams have children who are happier and have a greater sense of control over their destiny.

Talent, character, and a good sense of right and wrong are important. However, without a dream, without hope and motivation, a child is like a ship on dry land.

If your child has no direction, no hero, no dream, what do you do?

1. Look at yourself, and ask what is your dream? If the answer is, "I don't have one," that may be the problem. Get a dream, let your child have dreams.
2. If you feel that you are nurturing your child's dream, but your child seems to lack enthusiasm, ask yourself, "Is it my dream, or my child's?"
3. Inspire your child. After all, a good parent is an example, a great parent is an inspiration. Be an inspiration, a parent who nurtures dreams and hope.

2

The Game

The 2nd Life Lesson:
Keep in Focus the Goal of Children's Soccer

The morning dew had not yet burned off the soccer field as the sun rose over the San Gabriel Mountains. Each blade of grass lay tranquil and peaceful, ready to form the new carpet for tiny feet pushing a leather ball around in hopes of scoring a goal. I looked proudly at my son, Vinnie, who had just turned five. Glimpsed through the morning sun, he looked somewhat like a Raggedy Andy doll: oversize shorts extending halfway down his calves, shin guards dangling from his socks like Roman shields, and a shirt that was at least five sizes too big with baggy sleeves draped over his fingers. But the one thing that fit just perfectly was his huge grin. His little thumping heart was full of expectations.

I, too, took a deep breath. I could smell a faint hint of orange blossom mixed with freshly cut grass that made the experience complete. This was no baseball field, but I had the same excited feeling and anticipation of fun and adventure that

I had when I played Little League baseball. His two younger siblings, Kaycee and Michael, stood with their mom on the touchline. I knew little about the sport, though my family is from Italy, home of some of the greatest soccer players in the world.

Vinnie's coach, Hank, a burly, angular man, looked like every baseball coach I had ever seen, except he was dressed in shorts rather than trousers and wore a red bandanna instead of a baseball cap. But he had that same authoritative strut and command to his voice that I'd seen around every baseball diamond. Our team, the Bears, was preparing to face the Hornets. I looked over to the other side of the field where the Hornets were huddled. Three of the boys perched on a soccer ball, using it as a pogo stick to bounce around on their little rear ends, then fell on the ground, rolling in the dirt and doing what kids do best: having fun. They didn't look much like Hornets to me. Hank, whose nickname I would not discover until later, led our five-, six-, and seven-year-olds through a vigorous calisthenics routine. Quite impressive, I thought, despite the fact that they were all hopping up and down, much to Hank's displeasure, like spilled marbles bouncing along the ground.

The Game

Then the game began. It looked nothing like the games I'd seen on TV, with the players spread across the field in a neat order, the ball passing between them methodically. This was more like a game of rugby, with everyone swarming after the ball, kicking it, missing, diving, and falling on the ground. A few kids appeared to have some skill, but the majority were just expressing the freedom of being outside, kicking and jumping and having a great time.

The score at the end of the first half was 1–1. As they walked off at halftime all the little boys had big smiles that could light up a moonless night. Then Hank began his halftime pep talk. He loomed over the Bears and shouted, "What is wrong with you? Why don't you listen? Stay in your positions and you forwards, don't just dribble the ball, *shoot!*" In an unforgiving tone he urged them to, "Be more intense. More intense. More intense." The kids looked up at him with furrowed brows, confusion etched across their faces.

I couldn't help noticing the Hornets' coach, Judy. She was kneeling down, eye level to her players, smiling and laughing with them.

As the whistle blew for the start of the second half, I was astonished to hear Hank whisper to our gangly striker, Shawn, "If their number 6 gets in your way again, take him out." What did that mean? As the second half began I noted that Judy had substituted in her second team, giving every child a chance to play, and luckily the no. 6 had been left out. We, however, still had in our starting eleven. It quickly became apparent that their second team was no match for our first. Only their goalkeeper, Armando, an obviously talented kid, remained in, but he alone was no match for our forwards, especially Shawn. The second half was barely a minute old when our Bears scored.

As the game restarted, the Hornets' goal quickly came under attack again. Little Armando worked valiantly, diving to the left and right, blocking shots, scampering across the goal mouth, throwing his body in the way of the ball. But his effort was in vain and a third goal came within a couple of minutes. The Hornets' entire defense seemed to have melted with the substitution of their key players. Every time the ball hit the back of the net, Hank jumped into the air, landed on his knees, arms outstretched, and yelled "Gooooooal!" at the top of his lungs.

After the fourth goal blasted past him, poor Armando's spirits withered. His shoulders slumped, his arms hung listlessly by his sides. "You couldn't catch a cold," shouted one of the Little Bears' dads.

Armando's dad, José, was easy to pick out from the crowd. He was the man with the anguish in his face. A muscular, square-jawed man with olive skin whom I judged to be hardworking by the calluses and fine scratches etched across his hands, he shouted the first words of encouragement to his son, "Great try," "Good effort," and "That's my son." His words were filled with warmth, acceptance, and support. But as each goal was scored, his voice strained. "Watch out! Man on the right!" His cross expression clearly said, "Why are they allowing this to happen to my son?" The same thoughts were racing through my mind. Why didn't Hank substitute some of our players to even the game out? Yes, we were winning, but at what cost? The game as a competition was over. Now it was the slaughter of the innocent. Somebody had made a mistake. Now all the Hornets' parents swarmed around their coach, yelling at her, urging her to "do something."

Then it happened. The sixth goal shot past Armando and he sank to his knees, all seven years of him, tears streaming down his face as he realized how hopeless it all was now. But in kids' soccer, the game is not played just on the field, but also on the touchlines. I could see Armando's mother holding onto his father's arm. She pleaded, "Don't go, you'll only make things worse for him."

But José could not be deterred. He tore out onto the field, picked up his son, and hugged him. Everyone heard it. "Dad, I tried, I tried. I can't stop them. I'm no good."

Then José replied, "Son, I love you. I love you. Now don't give up. Don't give up." Then he looked up and glared at Hank, anger and anguish glistening in his eyes. He didn't say anything. Hank and the Bears could have their victory. All he wanted was for his son not to be hurt anymore. I looked at the Hornets' baby faces that had been filled with bouncing giggles an hour ago. Now, half their light was out, their spirits crushed.

Then Hank did the unthinkable and yelled at Armando's tearful father. "Get off the field, we're not finished with you yet. Losers cry. Winners win," he mocked. "No wonder your kid cries with the example you give him."

José walked slowly over to Hank. Everyone stared in stunned silence as José raised his fist, his eyes fixed on Hank. Then, just as suddenly, José lowered his fist and gently shook his head. "And what are you really winning?" he asked Hank. "If it means that much to you, take the victory. If beating up little boys is what you call winning." He turned to go back to his wife, carrying his son. At that moment, it was as if dark clouds and evil spirits overshadowed the blue sky. Parents turned on coaches, parents on parents, team on team, coach on coach. Good manners and good sportsmanship were bid good riddance for the rest of the season.

A parent of one of the Hornets yelled out that he thought they needed a "real coach." Another cried, "Hey, Judy, get our good players—like my son—back on the field instead of these goofs!"

"Who are you calling a goof?" responded another wounded Hornets' parent. A scream across the field followed. "We'll show you who's not done scoring. If Armando's dad's afraid to knock your block off, I'm not, you *#@*%*#!!!"

Hank puffed out his chest and shouted back, "After we kick

another goal past you, I'll be over there to kick your *#@*%*#!"
He looked down for the adulation of his Bears but all he saw
were three boys with their fingers in their ears and the rest
frowning. This was the first time some of the children had been
exposed to such hatred demonstrated by anyone, let alone their
moms and dads.

The damage had already been done. What at first had been
a great day for kids had become a nightmare, a bitter feud
between parents and coaches. And it was unlikely to end there.
The incident had brought out the worst aspects of human
nature and would set the tone for the rest of the season. What
happened?

Children May Be Children, But Parents and Coaches Should Behave Like Adults

I realized that the problems with soccer were no different from
those I'd encountered in Little League. The most surprising
thing about kids' sports is that the parents can be reduced to
barbarianism much more easily than their children. Players and
parents who arrive with open hearts and smiling faces, eager to
learn and have fun together, can be soured by adults who've forgotten the true meaning of soccer or any children's sport.

The goals of youth soccer are simple and fourfold: for the kids
to have fun, to be safe, to build character, and, most important, to
learn sportsmanship and fair play. At my son's game, the adults,
the guardians of those principles, had failed the children. What
struck me even more than the adults' immaturity was that it took
only one man to initiate the conflict, which was fueled by the

other adults, myself included. I'd cheered and jumped for joy after each goal. I urged our boys to score more and I certainly didn't go to Hank and say, "Hey, this is unfair." I reveled in the other team's defeat. I felt stronger and superior because my team—my son's team—was mauling another bunch of five- and six-year-olds. *Sad,* I thought, is not the word. *Tragic* was more like it.

And why do we adults allow this behavior to continue? The reason is simple. We have forgotten what is important. We all want our children to be made of the "right stuff," to be confident, happy. But the right stuff is not created overnight. We forget that scores are meaningless to a child. What builds the right stuff is not winning, not being the best, but *trying* one's best. Never giving up. That's the message we should be instilling in our children. That's the lesson that will best serve them throughout their lives. But to do this correctly we must be as concerned for another parent's child as for our own—even if that child is on the opposing team. Empathy and the ability to have compassion and protect all the children, not just your own, is the life lesson that will help our children most.

I Have Met the Enemy, and the Enemy Is Me

As everyone left the field that day, not even the victors seemed to feel good about themselves. Our coach, Hank, smiled, but it was a shallow and embarrassed one. I stared at him, appalled with the way he had fashioned the game, and I was going to have to air my disgust. It was unsportsmanlike and unfair to the kids, to say the least. In fact it was outrageous arrogance. He had single-handedly destroyed the game for everyone. That's what I'd tell him.

I walked over to him and the words just fell out. "Great job, coach."

I couldn't believe that I'd just reinforced his destructive behavior. How many times has any parent done that? Each time my child comes back from a game, what is the first thing I ask him? Did you win? Did you score a goal? Is that really what I should be asking? Only one team ever wins, so there is a 50 percent chance that he is going to have to embarrassingly admit, "No, I lost, Dad. I'm a loser." Usually only one or two players at most will get to score a goal during a soccer match. Defenders, even good ones, might not score during an entire season. And in fact, is winning and scoring goals the reason why they're there, or is it something else? Something that provides a victory even in defeat? Something that is more enduring than just talent, the scoreboard, or the standings? Something that makes children the *right stuff*?

So, instead of, "Did you win?" or, "Did you score a goal?" what should we be asking? How about, "Did you have fun?" or, "What did you do?" The score isn't the important part and it's a fallacy to say that winning breeds success. After all, winning is usually never final and losing is never fatal.

To top it all off, as I walked to my car, I overheard Richard, a Hornets dad, talking to his son. "A woman for a coach— damn, we'll never win. She keeps you, her best player, out and puts in kids that can't kick the dirt let alone the ball." I thought that Judy was a good coach who had ensured that all her players played. Now she was being vilified for doing the right thing. That's why so many good coaches quit. I didn't realize it at the time, but Hank had made it look as if he'd substituted his best player. But he merely got Shawn, our top scorer, to switch shirts with another boy, so he could stay in the game! That's right, all hail the motto "Win at all costs."

I remember my father's words when I was first teaching my kids to play ball. He put his hand on my shoulder and said, "Vin, there is no doubt that you have learned to win in life. But you did that not by winning but by something else." He reminded me of the adage: "Winning and talent will get your kids to first base, but it is their character and how they deal with losing that will bring them home." The metaphor is a little mixed when applied to soccer, but the spirit of the saying is exactly the same.

But what is character and how do you build it? Can parents and coaches influence children to grow up to be the right stuff? Can they foster a child's self-esteem and inner security? Certainly I saw during the game that day how parents and coaches can do exactly the opposite and destroy children's confidence and self-esteem. Which begs one question above all others: why?

From the Doctor's Desk

The major reasons why adults cause youth sport to deteriorate into a competition among adults are:

1. An instinctive, primal need for a parent to protect a child from what the parent perceives as the pain of losing.
2. Unconscious expectations of parents and coaches.
3. Confusing success for children with success for parents.
4. Parents' lack of know-how when it comes to positively influencing their child.

Primal protection, probably the most powerful of all emotions, is the instinctive force that drives a parent to protect his child at all costs. It is so powerful in women that when given a choice between saving either their child or their husband, 98 percent of more than two thousand women surveyed said they would save the child. Only 52 percent of men said they would save their child over their spouse, according to an Adelphi University study. José's first instinct was to protect his son by running onto the field.

Unconscious parental and coach expectations take on many aspects. The day we think we have *no* hang-ups is the day we just added another. We have expectations that we don't even realize we possess. Fathers and mothers unconsciously believe, "My son or daughter must be everything I was not," or, "She must be as great as I think I am." Coaches have dreams of grandeur, of being "the winner." They fear being rejected by the parents as a failure if they don't win. Later chapters will be devoted to this issue.

Confusion about what success is for a child versus success for an adult stems from parents and coaches experiences where they are evaluated on results only. Who cares how hard one worked, studied, or tried—you either got an A or not. Even in *Star Wars*, the wise old Jedi, Yoda, said, "There is no *try*. Only *do!*" However, for children, success is effort, trying hard, never giving up. Many parents are surprised to learn that results for children are minor. The fast track to childhood failure is to praise only results.

Most parents, although well intentioned, do not know how to influence their children to try their best and never give up. Perseverance is taught, fostered, and nurtured by you, the parent. Hank's answer to the problem was that the team must be "more intense." But he wasn't teaching them about perseverance, the means to an end; he was simply focused on the goal.

Remember: You can open the door for your child but you cannot make him walk through it.

PART I

THE KEYS TO SUCCESS

Children Are Not Born All at Once, But Bit by Bit

Every parent wants the same thing for his or her children: for them to be successful winners in life—a Pelé, a Michael Jordan, a Tiger Woods, an Einstein, a Mother Teresa. But none of these people were born the way we remember them. Confidence, self-esteem, the "right stuff" are not genetically inherited. They are carved out bit by bit, chiseled like Michelangelo's *David* from a pristine slab of marble. Every major study in the past decade shows parental influence is essential for a child's success. Biological research has shown conclusively the brain's capacity and a child's ability can be increased by certain mental and physical experiences.

There are essential ingredients—I call them keys—that parents can use to help their children reach their goals. They are:

1. Communication
2. Presence
3. Attitude
4. Acceptance

Parents can be either a help or a hindrance to their child's success. Parents can instill either self-confidence or fear, honesty or deceitfulness, courage or cowardliness, discipline or irresponsibility, loyalty or selfishness. Soccer provides an essential opportunity to instill these principles.

Remember, children are like newly fallen snow: Be careful what you do, because every mark will show.

3

Communication

The 3rd Life Lesson:
Say and Do What You Mean, and Listen to Your Child

The Key That Makes First Contact

Communication is the bridge that brings a child and parent together. The word *communication* in Latin means "to come as one." There are two basic steps to communicating: talking and listening. Before you can teach, you must communicate.

My relationship with my children demonstrates the divisions in communication as well as any. They are computer literate, I am not. They understand all the terms used in soccer, I do not. Or didn't. In fact, when I first heard the term *striker,* I thought, why would we want one on our team? We already had enough people not working. And we certainly didn't need anyone striking out. Of course, the term *striker* applies to the team's target man, the primary goal scorer, and is obviously an excellent person to have on a team. But it just goes to show how the same word or phrase can have totally different meanings to kids and adults. This gulf in communication became very apparent in the second game of the Bears' season.

I arrived early to find that a tent had been set up on our side of the field, which I presumed was there to keep the sun off the players. As Hank, the coach, marched onto the field he looked around for the kids but couldn't find them. They were all in the tent. He yelled angrily at them to get out. "Now. Move it, move it. Get out of there. You should be warming up, not sitting around in tents. Get out!"

Eric Woo, an impish boy who played left back and had an almost permanent smile etched on his face, sheepishly poked his head out and in genuine puzzlement said, "But, Coach, in the last game you yelled at us that we were not *in tents* enough." Hank exploded and yelled even louder, screaming unintelligible expletives at the terrified boys. As for me, I couldn't stop laughing.

Sarcasm Scars—Say What You Mean

"Oh, yeah, very clever, Woo. You're a very clever boy." Hank was marching behind little Eric, snarling sarcastically. The boy's expression was a picture of bemusement. They had done what the coach had told them—been *in tents*—and now the coach was clearly angry but still telling him he was smart. He didn't understand. Was he good or bad? He obviously couldn't work it out. And he looked like he just wanted to cry.

What most coaches and parents don't understand is that children, especially those under seven, interpret things literally. They are also egocentric; that is, they believe that whatever happens around them somehow had something to do with them. Eric misinterpreted the word *intense*, thinking it meant "in tents," and he and many of the other children felt they were in some way responsible for the acrimony during and after the game. By the age of ten most children understand there are events that occur for which they are not responsible. In fact, any parent of an adolescent might think they take no responsibility for anything. I assure you, they do.

Time and Space Are Two-Dimensional

While watching TV soccer reruns, my son Vinnie said to his four-year-old brother, Michael, "I bet your candy bar that Cobi Jones scores from that free kick."

Michael weighed it up for a moment, then nodded. "OK. I bet he doesn't."

Jones stepped up to take the kick and sure enough bent the ball round the wall and into the net. As Michael went to hand over the candy bar, Vinnie admitted, "I cheated. I saw him score it yesterday on the news."

Michael quickly replied, "So did I but I never thought he could do it again."

Events and time for a child under seven are often one-dimensional, and two separate events, though remembered, are not connected. This is why, when instructing a child, we must repeat, repeat, and repeat. Practice makes perfect. It is not that they are not listening, it's that their "computer" has not yet booted up completely. We've all experienced the, "Mom, are we there yet?" asked every five minutes on a trip.

At a pizza parlor, I asked Michael if he thought the world was round or flat. He answered with certainty that the world was round *and* flat.

"That's impossible, Michael," I said. "It must be either round or flat. It can't be both." Michael shook his head and pointed to our pizza.

Depth perception, volume, and many spatial relations are concepts that we take for granted, but sometimes a child's two-dimensional concepts are difficult to refute. Remember: Children under nine literally don't see or recognize things as adults do, so we must take that into account. Children's developing neural circuits, together with their underdeveloped sight, hearing, and brain senses, make them see and interpret things differently. I remember the first time my dad bought me a microscope. For months afterward, I continually washed my hands, afraid of the world of little creatures I had seen that I never before knew existed.

Seventy-three percent of kids quit their childhood sports by age thirteen because, according to studies, it ceases to be fun, and the pressures put on them by coaches and parents don't make sense to them and don't make it worthwhile. To avoid these problems it is important that parents and coaches recognize and account for the differences in understanding and communication between adults and children. They simply are not the same. Say what you mean and mean what you say. Sometimes that means you must draw it out and make certain your child understands your terminology. Never assume anything.

Children Do What We Do

Charlie, excited after his game, asked his father, "Can we go to get ice cream now, Dad?"

Charlie's dad replied, "Yo!"

Charlie looked questioningly at him. "Is that yes or no, Dad?"

"You heard me. Yo!"

Charlie's voice turned into a whine. "Please, Dad, please. Is that yes or no?"

"Yo!"

Luckily Charlie's mom came to the rescue before Charlie broke down in tears. "Stop being stupid, Sam. Yes or no?"

"Yo!" he yelled again. At that point I just wanted to go over and get involved, but I refrained. Interestingly, I had heard Charlie saying exactly the same thing to his younger sister at training two days earlier. Yes, we teach our children many things, even how not to communicate. Such frustration is the first ingredient of failure.

Because adults understand the subtleties of language, they can use it in a sophisticated way. But kids often can't understand what is being said. When adults don't validate a child's insight, they begin to lose confidence in their perceptions. It's like a teacher marking you wrong for all your correct answers. That is what happens when adults use sarcasm, cynicism, or any glib remark where the words do not carry the meaning.

I remember being so confused at my first baseball game when I missed an easy fly ball that bounced in and out of my glove. My coach yelled, "Great catch. Next time use glue." I remembered the tone wasn't very nice and clearly told me that I was bad. Children judge everything as either good or bad, something that pleases you or displeases you. They don't get that you are just being a wise guy. They just perceive you as being really mean, and yes, childish. As much as they want to play with you, they also look to you to be the adult.

Children See What We Say

Many children are easily distracted when not in the fray of the game. As the Hornets' Francis dribbled the ball upfield toward the goal, Charlie, our center back, was busy watching the grass grow. He didn't even notice Francis sweep right past him. Hank yelled at Charlie, "Great defending!" It sounds positive, but let's add what we call "the process," the tone of voice and body language: angry and shouting, kicking the dirt.

More than just words convey our message. It is always the process that does it. In bringing a child across the bridge we must make the way simple and clear. Communication takes completely different forms for children and adults. For adults, a message is conveyed 80 percent by the words and 20 percent by the body language and tone of voice used. For children, tone and the body language communicate 90 percent of the message. The words are much more often misinterpreted or misunderstood. The first communication between you and your child was your eyes meeting, then you smiled and she smiled. If you spoke loudly or angrily, she pouted or cried. Listen to anyone talking to a child in a singsong voice. Childlike, we call it. And then somewhere along the line we suddenly think they're adults. We urge them when toddlers to talk and to get up and walk. When they do, too often we then tell them to sit down, behave, and be quiet. Yes, it's confusing.

Listen!

The following story illustrates a parent who talks but does not listen.

Ralph, the wily, freckled goalkeeper of the Hungry Hawks, signaled to his coach midway through the second half of a closely fought game. "Coach, Coach," he cried out as his team was attacking the Bears' goal. The chubby coach peered over his spectacles and the little boy crossed his legs and screwed his face up in anguish. The coach ignored him and tapped his watch. It was close to the final whistle.

After several minutes of constant pressure on the Bears' goal, the Hawks finally scored to take a 2–1 lead. All the players and parents jumped up and down in celebration. All except Ralph, who was standing between the posts with his legs still firmly crossed, not daring to move, much less bounce. "Coach, Coach. Please . . ." he cried out again with a long drawn out "please."

"Not now," the coach shouted back. "We're ahead."

The Bears took the kickoff and played the ball out wide to the right. After some fierce tackles, the ball finally broke loose to the Bears' right-winger, Carlos, who chipped the ball into the middle of the Hawks' half of the field. Shawn, the Bears' striker, raced onto it as two Hawks defenders scampered back. Shawn reached the ball first and looked up toward the Hawks' goal. All the players, coaches, and parents followed his gaze and were amazed to see not Ralph in the Hawks' goal, but his three-year-old brother, Kevin, who had heard Ralph's pleas and come to the rescue.

As Shawn approached with the ball, Kevin dived at his feet, tackled his leg, and hung on while Shawn tried to shake him off. But where was Ralph? Then everyone turned around at the loud flushing sound coming from the clubhouse. The door swung open and Ralph trotted back out to the field, tying the string at the front of his shorts, totally oblivious to the fact that everyone was staring at him. He reached his goal, pulled his gloves back on, and looked up. "Let's go!" he shouted, clapping his hands enthusiastically. The referee scratched his head, bewildered. He didn't know whether to pull out a yellow card for a warning, a red card for an ejection, or maybe just a joker card.

Parents, Be Consistent—Send Out One Message Together

We parents, coaches, and referees must listen to our kids. It is our obligation. Just because they are small, what they say is just as important to them as our words are to us. In fact, the majority of the people who are considered good lecturers say that they believe their parents really listened to them. Listening makes your child feel important, and that will encourage him to communicate, because he will feel you're hearing his views and ideas.

Duty and Imagination

"Maria, remember you're a fullback. You have to stop their forwards from scoring," urged the Blue Bells' coach, Hope.

"OK, Coach," Maria replied with a grin. Two minutes later Maria was way out of position at the other end of the field with the other girls, dribbling and shooting and twirling her curls. Nonetheless, Maria managed to score a goal. Her teammates congratulated her and she ran back to her position at the back for the kickoff.

This time Hope was more specific. She was Maria's first-grade teacher as well as her soccer coach, so she reminded her of something they had discussed in class. "Maria, remember the story of the Alamo, where Davy Crockett never left his position, not for any reason?"

"Yes," said Maria.

"Well, be like Davy Crockett and stay there at all costs. Got it?"

"Got it, Coach," beamed Maria. The game continued and Maria maintained her position. Hope's communication was simple and direct and it worked. She said it at eye level, maintained good eye contact, and spoke in terms that Maria could understand.

Shortly after the game, they all returned to the locker room. An hour later Hope was headed out to her car when something caught her attention out of the corner of her eye. Maria was still standing on the field in the fullback position. If she hadn't been retrieved she may have stayed at her post forever. What devotion. What power our suggestions can have.

Most of us do not understand how important our approval is to our children. What we mean as mere suggestions or rules are often taken as "missions" to children in their attempts to please us and earn our approval. If our approval is reasonably and consistently obtained, children develop a certitude and confidence in how to deal with situations. If they do something and are rewarded, they start to feel even more confidence and that they are in control of their lives. Parents and coaches who have expectations that are not congruent with the child's ability can take even the most highly motivated child and drain him or her of all confidence and self-assurance. They become quitters. And quitting is probably an appropriate mechanism to remove the child from a situation where he is only going to fail, and feel terrible about himself.

Two Instructions Too Many

Remember that children take things literally.

I was at the end of my tether. I was no longer coaching with Hank and my team was playing the Bears. They had scored two goals in as many minutes, simply because my defenders, the Blizzards, were chasing the ball into midfield instead of keeping their positions in defense. Derrick and Tony (nicknamed Two-Ton because of his size) seemed to be magnetically drawn to the soccer ball and each time they were pulled out of position, we conceded a goal. What made the situation worse was that the Bears were coached by Hank and as ever, he really brought out the competitive spirit in me. I didn't want to lose this game.

At halftime I called my nine-year-old center backs Derrick and Two-Ton over and drew huge circles in our half of the field. "Stay in these circles until the ball comes into our half," I told them. "Then you can leave the circles and go after the ball. Understand?" They both looked up at me and nodded unequivocally.

The second half, my Blizzards really took it to Hank, I mean, the Bears, but within a few minutes the Bears broke from defense and Shawn, their striker, raced with the ball at his feet toward Two-Ton. Tony ran to block his route to goal but then all of a sudden stopped dead, as if he'd been pulled back by a chain. Shawn was left one-on-one with our goalie and as he slotted the ball past him, I dropped to my knees in despair. The parents on the touchline stared in bemusement, but of course only I knew why he'd suddenly stopped and let Shawn run unchallenged toward the goal.

Tony had remembered only half of my command, the part where I told him to "stay in the circle," and he had taken me literally. Many children this age cannot follow compound instructions—the message doesn't stick in their memories. As a neurologist, I should have realized that the memory development of nine-year-old children means that they take what you say literally and remember only half of what you say at best.

 From the Doctor's Desk

1. Use simple language.
2. If possible, always talk to children at eye level, making eye contact as you did when they were infants.
3. Make certain your tone of voice and body language convey the same message as your words.
4. Listen, listen, listen, especially to their tone of voice and any facial expression they make. It tells you what they are really saying and its urgency or importance.
5. Never underestimate the importance of your request, nor a child's imagination.
6. Spatial relations and time concepts are often not fully matured until the age of eleven.
7. When teaching, say it, do it, and repeat it.
8. Children feel responsible when they perceive you are upset. Explain your moods to them and tell them when they are not the cause.

The first key inserted makes contact. Now, let's use the second key that unlocks the door and can lead our children to success.

4

The Present

The 4th Life Lesson:
Be Present in Body and in Mind

I once overheard my daughter talking to my youngest son, Michael, about the nature of time. She was only seven, but spoke with an authority beyond her years. "You see, Mike, the past was yesterday, like when we went to the store with Daddy to buy the soccer ball. And the future is tomorrow, when we're supposed to go to the beach. But today is a gift. That's why we call it the present."

I was somewhat astounded when I heard her say this. I had never quite thought of time in that way. But when I'm on the touchline at a soccer game I think that most people seem to have forgotten what time is really about. There's no time to watch their child's game, there's no time to look into their child's eyes, to see his smile. And more important, there's no time for the child to look into his parents' eyes and recognize just how important he is to them. Only when children grow older do you realize that for them the sun rises and sets on their parents' approval. And anybody who has teenagers realizes that that changes completely with adolescence. Parents become nothing more than a steady downpour on their children's heads and they will do anything to avoid them. So we as parents have only a small window, a small precious gift of the present, to experience the adoration and influence in our children's lives. That time for fathers is generally when their children are between five and twelve years old and for moms maybe a little longer, from birth to about fourteen.

The Present Is a Gift—So Is Your Child

I'll never forget Frankie, a six-year-old. He would arrive at each soccer game with his mom and dad, who would always drop him off and then leave. I felt a little sorry for Frankie. I always thought that he could be a much better player if only his parents would stick around and watch. I knew that his dad must love him because I would frequently see them around town, with Frankie tightly gripping his dad's hand. I just couldn't understand why he never stayed for the games.

I usually didn't start Frankie in the game, since I always tried to reward those parents who stayed to support their kids and, to be fair, Frankie wasn't one of the better players. I feel a little chagrin now for admitting that. But one day he came up to me and said that he wanted to start the game and play both halves. I was a little puzzled and when I asked him why, he replied: "Well, today my dad will be able to see me play for the first time."

I looked around and saw his mother on the touchline but not his father. I shrugged it off and decided to start Frankie anyway. He played superbly. He had never scored a goal before but netted two during that game. He played with spark, enthusiasm, and love for the game. After the final whistle I went over to his mom and said, "Frankie wanted to play the whole game because his dad was going to see him for the first time. But I don't see his dad anywhere."

His mother turned to me, choked back a tear, and said, "His dad died last week. The reason he never stayed for the games was because he was blind. And now Frankie knows that his dad is in heaven and can see him and can finally watch him play."

I was startled for a couple of reasons. First, my presumption that his dad didn't really care was way off the mark. And second, imagining his father's presence compelled Frankie to play so very well.

I think the same thing is true of other children whose parents come to games. In fact one coach I know did a survey and found that his team's goalkeeper allowed an average of only one goal a game when his parents were there and three when they were not. Similarly, his forwards' output was almost double that when their parents were there compared to when they were not. This reflects studies that were done at Yale and several other institutions in the seventies and eighties. When children were asked what was the most important thing that they remember about their experiences with Little League and school plays, 88 percent answered that it was either their parents' attendance or their lack of attendance. They rarely talked about winning teams or great plays. In a family therapy group I counsel, one parent, a renowned attorney who had sent his children to the best schools and given them every privilege that money can buy, was stunned when his son accused him of being a failure as a parent. Of all the soccer games he played in grammar school and high school, his father had attended only five. That's how his son had judged him.

Roger's Rock

Are rocks important? Are parents important? Stupid question?

"Hey, Dad, watch this," Roger cried out as he kicked the ball along the touchline as hard as his spindly legs could manage. Unfortunately, his father wasn't looking. Roger's dad was there only in body. His mind was, well, in the office, planning the room addition, fretting over the birds he saw pecking at his newly sown lawn that morning.

Roger grabbed his dad's hand. "I'll score a goal for you today, Dad. You watch, I'll score." His little face beamed up at his father, but his smile was lost on the cold granite stare of his dad.

The game kicked off and, standing by his words, Roger dribbled the ball downfield, winding in and out of the opposing defenders. It was desire rather than skill that propelled him toward the Amazing Aztecs' goal; it's remarkable what desire will do, even for a pint-sized little boy like Roger. But as he pushed the ball past the last defender between him and the goal, Roger suddenly stopped dead as if his engine had just run out of gas. The ball was immediately stolen from him, or rather just taken from him, and kicked back up the field toward the Bumble Bees' goal. As attention switched to the other end of the field, no one noticed Roger standing alone, staring forlornly toward the parking lot. No one heard him softly cry, "Dad, Dad. You said you'd watch, Dad."

With his head dropped, Roger turned away as his dad disappeared off into the distance to do "something important." An object on the ground caught little Roger's eye. He stooped down to pick it up and then stuffed it down his sock for safe-keeping. He ran back to join the game, but for the rest of the time he was no longer the same player. The desire had left him.

At halftime, I noticed him pulling the object from his sock. He opened his tiny hand and stared at the shiny black rock. He then whispered softly again, "Now you stay with me." And with a faint sigh he pushed the rock back down into his sock and turned his attention back to the coach's pep talk.

Each Child Wears an Invisible Sign That Reads "Make Me Feel Important"

A Painful Memory

The memory of a child is different from that of an adult. The present becomes the past not like a continuous video but more like a series of unconnected snapshots. They are mainly two types of childhood memories:

1. Exceedingly joyful events, such as opening a favorite birthday present.
2. Painful or sorrowful experiences.

This system of retrieving painful events has a purpose in survival terms: It maintains memories that prevent the child from being harmed again. A child bitten by a dog will often avoid pets as an adult. A child being injured when heading a soccer ball or deliberately left out of a game by a coach bent on winning are memories, snapshots that will affect whether the child views the game with like or dislike as an adult.

Most people asked to think back to childhood will often first remember the time they bumped their head, cut their finger, or were taken to the hospital. A parent disappearing from the sidelines when his child so wants him to be present will be stored in that child's memory as a snapshot.

Be there, be present—don't make sad, lonely memories for your child. The child's memories of a parent not being there at a game far outweigh his good memories.

From the Doctor's Desk

A parent's first step toward making his or her child a success is simply to be present at games. Just being there for the child is so important. Indeed, a child's self-esteem is based on three overriding factors:

1. Parental approval.
2. The child's own innate talent.
3. Peer approval.

Parental approval is most highly sought by preteens The time a parent spends with a child tells the child that he's OK, he's good, he's valuable, that he's worth your time. A coach, a sitter, or a teacher at this age are weak substitutes for a parent.

Your presence is essential.

Children don't understand that you need to work, and will often interpret your absence as meaning that work is more important to you than they are. Years down the road all they'll remember about the games are whether their parents were present. And when you think about it, what are you communicating to your child when you're not present? You may not mean it, but the message that comes across is, "You're not worth it."

I know parents are busy and feel their evenings and weekends are stretched thin between their responsibilities at work and their obligations to the family, but most of the time isn't that really just an excuse? When my employees tell me they have to leave work for a child's sporting event, I never think twice about letting them leave early. I believe that anybody who has the sense to put his family first is going to have an equally healthy attitude toward his job. I can trust and rely on these people, whom I know have the right sense of values. And most of the employers I know feel the same way.

Now the key that keeps the door wide open: attitude.

5

Attitude

The 5th Life Lesson:
Accentuate the Positive and Eliminate the Negative

It's What Lies Within, Not Without, That Counts

It was truly a once-in-a-lifetime experience. Dr. V. M. Fortanasce was early. Actually, I misread the schedule. Kickoff was at 10 A.M., not 9 A.M. Relieved to be an hour early rather than an hour late, I settled into the bleachers to watch the game that was finishing up.

I heard someone scream, "Enrico, concentrate. Stop dribbling and shoot!" The second half, it seemed, belonged to the Red Barons and Enrico was leading their attack. The coach screamed again, "Let's take it to them!" All eleven of the Barons looked like soldiers going into battle: no smiles, but expressions of determination. The score was already 3–0 to the Barons, who had dominated the first half.

Enrico was definitely talented for an eight-year-old and was all over the field, working hard in every position, as often occurs in kids' soccer. The T-Rexes, however, were attacking and looked certain to score when Enrico slid in to tackle the ball away just a couple of yards from his own goal line. He stood up to boot the ball clear, but as children frequently do, he took his eye off the ball and looked up the field for one of his own players. His kick completely missed the ball and he tumbled onto his back, landing on the ball, sending it rolling backward toward his own net. Enrico's goalkeeper stared in disbelief, frozen in shock, as the ball trickled past him and crossed the goal line. Enrico had scored for the opposing team. No one knew whether to cry or to cheer. Some parents weren't even sure if it counted—it's not as if you can score a home run for the wrong team in baseball, although I have seen a ball pop off Ken Griffey Jr.'s glove and fly over the fence for a home run.

That it was a goal became apparent to everyone when the cheers from the T-Rexes erupted like the rumble of thunder after the silence of bewilderment. "Enrico, you idiot!" That last word hung in the air, resonating over the field. Idiot, idiot, idiot. The Barons' coach kicked the dirt and knocked over a chair.

As the T-Rexes lofted the ball toward the Barons' defenders again, I gazed at their faces. No longer were they reflecting staunch determination; instead their expressions seemed to plead, "Oh, God, please don't let the ball come to me." By the time the game ended, the Barons crawled off the field 4–3 losers. Or was it their coach who was the loser?

It was time for my son's team to take the field. I was now an assistant coach to the indomitable "Hank the Horrible," as he was secretly known throughout the league. His insistence to "win at all costs," however, was becoming contagious, and other coaches were adopting his formidable style and vying for his position as the most winning, if infamous, coach in the league. It was not only the coaches but the parents as well who wanted to "win at all costs."

It was 9:45 A.M. and Hank strutted out for our game. I was helping by reminding him that these were not storm troopers but, well, just little soldiers. The game turned out to be a tightly contested battle, tied at 3–3 late in the second half. Our Bears chipped the ball into the Mighty Monkeys' penalty area, but one of their defenders coolly headed the ball back to his keeper, Brian, to clear it out. But as the ball was headed back to Brian, he suddenly noticed a frog in the penalty area. He forgot all about the ball bouncing toward him and instead picked up the frog.

He placed the frog safely off the field and then scampered back to the goal just as the ball bobbled to a stop a few inches from the goal line. Brian energetically dived at it, but rather than gathering the ball safely in his hands, his fingers accidentally pushed the ball over the line. Hank roared "Goooooaal!" and punched his fist into the air. There was then a hush and again many of the parents wondered if this counted as a goal. From the Mighty Monkeys' touchline their coach cried out, "That's OK, team. Brian, is the frog OK? Good dive, excellent try, Brian. Come on, team, heads up. Let's try for the equalizer." And the parents followed his lead and urged their kids on. "Go Monkeys, go!" Hank was silent for once.

When the game continued and once again the ball was lofted deep into the Monkeys' half, I looked at their defenders' faces. Clearly their expressions seemed to say, "God, please let the ball come to me."

That evening I reflected on the two games I had watched that day. What was the difference in each? In both games an error had been made, yet one team, when handed a lemon had turned sour, the other had just made lemonade.

An Event Is Neither Good Nor Bad, It's an Opportunity

One coach took the opportunity presented him and made a mistake into a disaster. The other took the opportunity to be positive and reward effort. The first coach filled his team with fear and taught them that errors are fatal. The other saw only a child's normal reaction and accentuated the positive and rewarded the boy's effort. Where one coach had used his key to lock out success, the other had used it to open the door to success.

It is our attitude, our unconditional regard, our focus on rewarding effort and illuminating an error that makes the difference between our child's eventual success or failure. Some parents are masters at taking an average child and instilling in him self-confidence. Others take the most talented children and scare the desire right out of them. Yes, children make errors, but twenty years from now, will it really matter about either goal? Well, yes, certainly, if you make it painful enough. Brian's smile after the game told the whole story. Yes, he'd be back. He loved the game and would try and try again. My dad once said: It's OK to lose, just don't lose the lesson.

From the Doctor's Desk

Parents need to remember that it's more important for children to learn how to lose than it is to learn how to win.

- Attitude is a decision.
- Those with the ability to see the good enable their children to see the good in themselves.
- Those who are rewarded for effort rather than for results learn to value the work ethic.
- Those who are treated as valued and precious begin to feel they can be effective.
- Those who feel they can change their world do, and never give up.

Being positive is not easy. It takes ingenuity and a decision. A decision to have a positive attitude.

Now the fourth and final key that invites your child to walk through the open door with confidence.

6

Acceptance

***The 6th Life Lesson:
There Is Only One Way to Accept Your Child:
Unconditionally***

Who's the richest man?
It is he who is content with what he has
—ALEXANDER HAMILTON

Sometimes someone else's parenting problem is so obvious that you wonder how they don't see it themselves.

Stevie's Dad

Stevie, at eleven, had a ton of talent: tall, muscular, fast, and agile with a built-in sense of ball control. His dad watched every game and regularly practiced drills with his son. He became known throughout the league as the "Superstriker," for his goal-scoring prowess. No one ever doubted who Stevie's father was.

He paced up and down the sidelines throughout every game. His voice stuck on one volume: very loud! I had a nickname for him: "Steaming Steve." At times he appeared ready to blow. Nothing but perfection from his son was enough. Despite the aggressive bellowing from his father, Stevie, however, always relied on his skill to beat opposing players and win matches, never resorting to cheating or dirty play. Intensity remained on his face from kickoff to final whistle. Unfortunately, there was rarely a smile.

In this particular game he had already scored three goals, but with the clock ticking down with seconds remaining and the Bears trailing the Stallions 4–3, he was sent clear of the last defender. Stevie took a single touch of the ball and chipped it over the approaching goalkeeper. The ball bounced once and struck the post and was deflected out for a goal kick. It was an easy chance for Stevie. As usual, just before he would bury the ball as he always did, his dad bellowed, "Spike it like I taught you!" As Stevie buried his foot into the ball, it shot out like a bullet, but missed wide by a foot. Not a sound was heard until the Stallions burst into cheers. I saw Stevie slumped on the ground, obviously crying. Stevie's miss had put the Bears out of the play-offs.

Even as Stevie walked off the field after the final whistle, his teammates patted him on the back. His father was uncharacteristically silent. Stevie approached his dad, smiling meekly, and shrugged, a gesture of regret on the one hand, and an attempt to have his dad console him on the other. What happened was unexpected. His father erupted. "What good are you, when your team really needs you, you let us all down! You walk around here with a smile on your face. It is a soccer game, not a beauty contest!" His dad turned and steamed off to the car. Stevie's face was flushed with embarrassment.

Although I love my son, I and every other parent watching secretly wished our children were as talented as Stevie (how easy they would have it). Despite Stevie's ability, he was always humble, never arrogant. His father made sure of that. Whatever he achieved on the soccer field, it always could have been better, faster, harder. Stevie's dad was a successful businessman who believed success came the hard way. When asked why he rode his son like he did, his comment was, "Life is dog-eat-dog, and I must prepare him." What Stevie's dad could not see was what he was doing to his son's confidence. He seemed never to accept his son, so his son never seemed content with himself.

Some parents think if a child is not the way they think he should be, then the child is not acceptable. They forget a child is an individual with his own personality. In fact, if Steaming Steve had some of his son's kindness and sincerity, I might have liked him. The fact is, I did not, nor did many other parents.

Daryl's Dilemma: Some Children Can't Grow Up Fast Enough

Daryl enjoyed playing in the under-ten soccer league until his parents manipulated their above-average nine-year-old son into the under-twelve-year-old league. For Daryl, even making the team was a huge achievement in itself. But that was not good enough for his parents' inflated egos. They forced him to leave his normal position as a defender and become first a midfielder and then a forward, so they could see him grab the goals and the glory.

Daryl had a lot of heart in dedicating himself to succeed in his new position. Being the smallest boy on the field, he was ultimately doomed to failure. He was felled by a lack of maturational development. He simply was not big enough. Daryl became despondent, believing that he would never be good enough. He frequently claimed stomachaches or forgot his cleats—anything to be excused from playing.

His discontented parents had spurned a self-critical child because they motivated him to satisfy them, rather than satisfy himself. These kinds of misguided parents tarnish gold with their dissatisfaction. They are never content with what they have, so they cannot see the treasure they have in their own child. These parents don't understand timely development. They are so anxious to have their child succeed (often to fulfill their own needs) that they fail to help him grow. Self-acceptance is as important to a child's psychological development as water is to a plant's growth. Without parental acceptance the child's psychological development will wither and his growth will be stunted.

Cassandra: Some Gifts Are Seen As Faults

Cassandra darted down the left wing with all the determination she could muster. As she passed me, I could see her enjoyment as her face beamed with a smile. Cassandra had that special something that makes me and her teammates like her. She was considerate, never pushing to be first on goal kick practice; always first to help gather the equipment up after the game or set things up for practice.

As the Blue Bonnet striker turned it on toward the goal, Cassandra seemed to slow down, almost as if to say, "Please, you go first." Her consideration for others, however, made her less aggressive, sometimes a liability in a competitive sport like soccer. Her mother, Debbie, was furious as she commented loud enough for me to hear, "What's wrong with you? You'll never make it." Her mother was oblivious to Cassandra's special gifts. Debbie was a social climber, a businesswoman. There is nothing wrong with that, but I felt it deterred her from appreciating Cassandra.

All children have their own personality traits, quirks, and tendencies. Some are aggressive and boisterous, or like to take charge. Others are shy, tender, and considerate. One is not better than the other. To Cassandra's teammates and opponents alike she was adequately talented, very sociable, and a considerate friend. To her mother, however, the same qualities that others admired she viewed as weaknesses. To Stevie's dad, his son's kindness was seen as an unmanly trait that would cause him ultimately to fail. Both Debbie's and Steaming Steve's comments and their demeaning tone of voice told their children, "Your personality is offensive. You are not acceptable." The gifts their children possessed were seen as faults. However, often I think that I did the same to my children. How could I be so blind? (We will talk more about this in the chapter on success.)

To achieve, children must believe. To believe, they have to be believed in. For young children parental acceptance is more important than any natural talent, however obvious.

Linda's Limp:
Where There's a Will, There's a Way

Linda was born with a hip problem that caused her to limp. She was awkward and clumsy both on and off the soccer field. But what she lacked in talent she made up in heart. Despite failure after failure, Linda approached every game, every tackle with unbridled determination and enthusiasm. She always tried the hardest, cheered and encouraged by her parents, and received a hug from them for that effort. Her attitude encouraged the whole team.

When I asked her father why his daughter seemed to be so well adjusted despite her lack of natural talent, he smiled and responded, "While I can't change the color of my daughter's eyes, I certainly can change the sparkle in them. I must accept what God gave me and treat it as a gift, and Linda is my gift."

Linda never noticed her limp, and neither did her parents. They did the three things necessary that communicate acceptance to a child:

1. Support a child's effort.
2. Validate her real accomplishments.
3. Affirm her worth.

Linda had everything against her from a physical standpoint, but everything for her from a parental one. Yes, parents can make the difference.

Corrective Action for Parents: Build Bridges, Not Walls

How can we help rather than hinder? Stevie's father could have affirmed Stevie's effort, telling him that few work harder than he. He could validate his accomplishments—he made three goals—and give him a high five. And then, if there were criticism, he could give it to him at that time. "The next time you're on one-on-one with the goalkeeper, get your foot around the ball to make sure you don't slice it wide." Stevie's father would then have been recognizing and appreciating Stevie's friendly sociable nature over a "win-at-all-cost attitude." At the same time, his father would have been able to make the loss and the missed shot a learning opportunity for Stevie, and ultimately helped him to be an even better player.

These opportunities also build a bond between parent and child. When your child is down, he will feel he can turn to you for advice. Why? Because no matter what the problem, he knows he will be accepted.

Acceptance is there in every parent. It takes no education, no extraordinary genetic talent, just common sense and diligence. If a parent accepts himself and is content with his child, his acceptance is reflected in the child. The child is self-satisfied. The child does not have to fulfill the parent's need, does not have to win to gain acceptance, but only has to try.

Parents' lack of acceptance is due to a misguided concept of themselves. For example, a parent who believes that he has not fulfilled his *own* parents' expectations may push his child to fulfill those goals, without even realizing it. Such parents tarnish their children with their arrogance and dissatisfaction. If parents do not accept their child and miss the opportunity to praise their efforts and accomplishments, a child will grow up not recognizing his own talents or believing in himself.

A Coach's Dilemma

Coaches need to recognize parents who do not accept their children and provide perspective to parents who are ready for a child to rocket to Mars even though he is not old enough to drive a car. A coach could ask Stevie's parents, "Are you satisfied with your son? If not, why not? He is the best in the league and he is having fun on the soccer field." To Daryl's parents, a coach could ask, "Do you see how incredibly hard your child tries? If not, why not? No one tries harder." Cassandra's mother could be asked, "Do you recognize Cassandra's special caring character?"

You might be thinking, "Isn't it the parents' problem? Should I interfere?" I say yes, if it is a repetitive problem affecting the child. As a coach you are more objective and can give them positive feedback. Try to intervene as close to the offending event as possible. Be kind but be firm. The parents will thank you for it.

From the Doctor's Desk

Accepting children without condition allows them to love themselves, see goodness in themselves, and give them confidence no matter what their talent. Before a parent can feel acceptance for her child, she must be able to accept herself.

A child's self-acceptance and self-confidence depends upon parents and coaches:

1. Accepting a child's ability.
2. Recognizing his age. It is better for a child to be a big fish in a little pond.
3. Always supporting a child's efforts.
4. Validating a child's true accomplishments.
5. Affirming their belief in a child's inherent worth to them.

6. Always empowering a child to feel he has the answers within himself.

Acceptance is so simple. It begins with the parents and coaches, the role models, and is absorbed by the child.

Contentment in the Adult Puts
Sunshine in the Child.

PART II

WHY YOU AREN'T USING THE KEYS

The four keys to success are simple. So why do things still seem to go wrong? The answer lies within us, the soccer parents and coaches. We are the wise adults.

It is our own unconscious and unrealistic expectations for our children to be more like *us:* to have the motor skills, aggression, intensity, focus, and seriousness that we would have if we were on the field, playing against our friends or business adversaries. Our basic instinct always to strive to be the best and the myth that a high IQ equates with happiness or success prevents us from using the four keys.

Remember, a person is successful when he gets what he wants, but he's only happy if he likes what he gets.

7

Expectations

The 7th Life Lesson:
All People Grow Older, but Some Never Grow Up

The Weight of Expectation

"Damn, Jimmy, kick it like I told you!"

"How could he miss that one?! Whose kid is that, anyway?"

"Open your eyes, referee! Or get a white stick!"

"My son's too good for this team. That's why he never scores—it's no challenge for him."

"Our team's ten times better than them. Someone must've paid the referee."

The game was not yet ten minutes old and already the parents and coaches were screaming, red-faced, from the touchlines. They screamed at each other, at the officials, and at their children struggling on the field. The camaraderie and the sense of fun that existed between the children as they playfully knocked the ball around before the game disappeared with the kickoff. Now the parents had taken over. Their demands and expectations had clouded the game and none of them could see it.

"Don't let him push you around!" another father screamed at his young son. If only they could hear themselves, I thought. Well, on one occasion I did get to listen to my own ranting from the touchline. Unknown to me, one parent had videotaped a soccer game I was coaching. At the end-of-season party, I had the misfortune to watch a screening of the tape. I paced up and down the touchline berating the referee, my players, and other parents— blaming everyone but the pope for our mistakes (and I have no doubt that if the pope had been there, I would have excommunicated him). It's true, I thought as I watched myself with increasing embarrassment. People get older, but some never grow up. All in all, I'd say watching that video put ten years on me. I could have won hands down the prize for the worst home video, a video that guaranteed my spot in soccer's hall of shame.

The Root of Parental Expectations

Now that we understand the four keys to success, what keeps us from using them? The main impediments, without doubt, are the unconscious (and sometimes conscious) expectations that parents and coaches hold. These expectations often stem from misguided concepts of how we parents view ourselves: who we think we are, or who we think we should be (but are not), and who we wish we were.

Children are often used as pawns to confirm or rectify the misguided perceptions their parents have of themselves. Since the most effective key to unlocking self-confidence within a child lies in parents accepting that child for who he is, the greatest example parents can set is to accept themselves, to believe in themselves. But they can only do that if they first *know* themselves and maintain a solid sense of humor in light of that knowledge. Parents pretending to be someone they're not can confuse and burden their children.

Parents and coaches must recognize and accept their own shortcomings. I've always noticed I have no problems receiving praise when it's due, only criticism when it's true.

We are how we were brought up. We are a combination of the early experiences we had with our parents and the later experiences with the peers we grew up with.

Who's Fooling Whom?

I remember the first soccer practice I attended. I had no intention of coaching, was too busy, and besides, I knew little about the game beyond recognizing the right moment to yell, "Gooooaaal!" Frank, one of the coaches, shook my hand and mentioned that I looked like I'd been an athlete. Before I could stop myself, I was rattling off my entire sporting résumé. "Captain of my Boy Scout troop, played varsity baseball, wrestled, won a couple of tennis titles, and, of course, was a gold medalist at the Junior Olympics." In one uninterrupted breath I had mentioned every sporting achievement including the blue ribbon I won for a bean bag race at age seven.

Frank's next question brought me crashing down to earth. "So, would you like to manage the equipment?" He must have noticed my expression drop and the color suddenly drain from my face. Then he asked, "You do know how to kick a soccer ball, right?"

"Of course," I scoffed, secretly thinking, How much different can a soccer ball be from a football?

And before I knew it, my mouth had run away with me again and I had talked myself into being assistant coach in a game I knew nothing about. Later in that season, I asked Frank why he'd singled me out to help him coach. "Your T-shirt had 'Notre Dame Coaching Staff' written on the back. I thought you would cry if I didn't ask you to coach!"

It always amazes me how we think we fool everyone around us with our affected behavior. Most people have summed us up within minutes of meeting us. The mask we wear covers only our face and fools no one else.

Yes, I was there for my son, but I was there even more for myself. I needed to be an integral part of this team. This need stemmed from my own childhood. As a kid, I was always the last one to be picked in team sports. In fact, the only reason I was ever picked at all was simply to keep the sides even. And now I was fulfilling that childhood desire to be picked first rather than last. Adults are nothing but children in grown-up clothes.

Who Are You?

While coaching and supporting youth soccer teams, I've keenly observed the parents of the young soccer players and found that they fall into six basic categories or personality types:

1. The overachiever parent.
2. The unfulfilled parent.
3. The overprotective parent.
4. The negligent parent.

5. The clueless parent.
6. The accepting parent.

1. The Overachiever Parent

In my social circles I seem to bump into a lot of big egos. At one party I said simply, "How's your daughter, Tina?" to Mrs. Bigwig and soon regretted it.

"Oh, she's marvelous," Mrs. Bigwig replied. "I don't know how she does it. Straight A student, captain of the soccer team. If she keeps this up she'll be another Bigwig with a Princeton scholarship."

"So," I said and smiled wryly, "will she be skipping second grade to go straight to third like my eldest son did?"

I quickly walked off before she had a chance to respond. The overachiever's motto is "You're never outdone as long as you get in the last word." I was as bad as she.

The overachiever parents are the braggarts. You know them by the nausea they provoke in those around them. Listen to them. If you substitute "she" and "her" for "me" and "my," you understand these people are not talking about their children, but glorifying themselves. "Look at my daughter, she's the best," really means, "Look at me, I'm the best."

Even if these parents have talented children, they raise such high expectations that the majority of their children fail. They don't ask their children, "Did you have fun?" but, "Did you score the winning goal?"

The overachiever parents use phrases such as "The best, the most, the superlative." Their children, on the other hand, say things like, "It's not fair. I should have done better." Their peers see them as intimidating or phony.

Parents who take themselves so seriously can cause their children to be nonaccepting and self-critical. For those who do become successful, they often turn out to be egotistical and judgmental. Others are often pessimistic and depressed.

2. The Unfulfilled Parent

A Man Is Content When Satisfied with What He Has

"Forty million just for an endorsement, that Tiger Woods has got it made," said José with astonishment to Coach Judy. "Imagine being his father."

In his youth José had been a gifted soccer player at a time when the best soccer players in the United States were unpaid amateurs. Now he worked hard at a factory nearby.

Ruben, a talented player, couldn't make a move on the soccer field without his father's commentary, urging and directing him. It was as if Ruben's very existence depended on the next pass, the next tackle, the next goal, the next game. Yes, José was present, but he was also a burden for Ruben.

In his haste to please his father, Ruben dangerously headed a low ball and received a glancing blow to the side of his head by an opposing player. The whistle blew and I ran out to see if he was seriously hurt. Ruben struggled up and, with tears of pain streaming down his cheeks, he assured me he was OK. "I can play," he said. "My dad would be upset if I didn't."

Some parents and coaches place enormous pressure on their children. What Ruben feared most was letting his father down. He knew how much his playing—and playing well—meant to his dad. Ruben was there for his father, his father was there for himself.

The unfulfilled parents are those who weigh down their children. They have forgotten that soccer is for their child's development, not their own. They don't understand that they cannot live their children's lives and their children cannot heal their childhood wounds.

The unfulfilled parents use phrases such as, "You have to, you must, don't forget, watch out." Their children say things like, "I'm sorry for letting you down." Their peers often feel sorry for them.

Children with unfulfilled parents often give up or become depressed. Those talented enough go on to become "enablers," taking responsibility for everyone else's happiness. These parents fail to separate their needs from their children's and do not accept their status in life. They often convey a negative attitude and have four criticisms for every one encouraging remark. Their children rarely gain self-esteem because a child cannot fulfill a parent's need for self-acceptance.

3. The Overprotective Parent

Sarah was always sick, sorry, and sad—but very sweet. When the ball skidded out of play on a wet pitch, Sarah was the nearest player to retrieve it and take the throw-in. She looked over at her mother on the touchline. Her mother frowned and shook her head. "You won't be able to throw it in, Sarah. It's too hard. The ball's too wet. Let someone else do it."

In the next game, when Sarah's mother wasn't there, I encouraged Sarah to try taking a throw-in. She refused. "I can't do it," she whispered. "I can't get it right."

The overprotective parents constantly make decisions for their children, leaving them perpetually insecure.

The overprotective parents use phrases such as, "You can't do it, it's too hard, I'll do it for you." Their children say things like, "I couldn't help it, I can't," and their peers often ignore them. They usually can only make friends with other victims. Frequently, in later life, they pick partners who abuse them. They play the eternal victim. The key not being used here is positive attitude. Again the parents' problem is one of self-acceptance.

4. The Negligent Parent

Brian's bright face paled as he watched his father leave. Neither of his parents ever stayed to watch their son play soccer. He played every game for three seasons and trained every week, but his parents were never on the touchlines. Despite the continual disappointment, Brian would arrive for every game and without fail ask his parents, "Are you going to watch me play?" His dad always had some excuse. He had to clean the garage, service the car, play golf with his boss. His mother's favorite response was, "I work all week. I need to take ten minutes to have my nails done."

The negligent parents are self-involved, self-indulgent, and narcissistic. They hide behind the veil of responsibility.

The negligent parents use phrases such as, "I have other obligations, you're not the only one, I can't do everything."

Their children's words are spoken through their sad, solemn faces.

Their children rely on their own abilities and if they make it in life, it's no thanks to their parents. These children need good coaches. The key these parents fail to use is presence. The negligent parent forgets child rearing takes effort, sacrifice, and, most important, requires making the child a priority.

5. The Clueless Parent, Perfect but Unreal

An Interesting Phenomenon Is How Heads Swell When They Stop Thinking

Mr. Sherman's outfit said it all. He was dressed in a dress shirt, shorts, black ankle socks, and polished brogues. He marched over to me and announced in a clipped English accent, "I picked your team for my son Reginald to play in because I heard you were the best coach. I used to play professional soccer in England. With the right coaching, Reginald can do the same. He plays center forward."

We began shooting practice, with each child taking shots at the goal. To this day I can picture little Reginald's stony expression, his face filled with fear. He was an average-sized boy for his age but was devoid of that mischievous streak that most boys his age seem to possess. Reginald never smiled and took everything very seriously. Too seriously.

As he ran up to shoot the ball, I felt a deep pang in my stomach because I wanted him to do well. But his shot flew yards wide of the post. "Reginald, how could you!" shouted his dad, grabbing his son's arm and scolding him in front of the rest of the team. Reginald seemed to melt into the ground. I'm sure he just wanted to vanish into thin air.

By the time practice was over, Reginald had missed every shot and Mr. Sherman ("Sherman Tank" as he'd quickly become known) had berated not only his son but also the *terrible* condition of the field, the air pressure of the ball, and the ability of the coaching staff whom he now believed had been "grossly overrated." The manager and I felt run over by the Sherman Tank.

I saw poor Reginald sitting alone, his head drooping, dejected I felt sure by his father's outbursts. I felt sorry for him, realizing he had to contend with his father daily. I placed a reassuring hand on his shoulder but was shocked when he threw my hand off and shouted, "You don't like me! How could I kick *that* ball on this *terrible* field?!"

Alas, like father like son. His father refused to accept the obvious, that his son needed lots of practice. To Mr. Sherman, blame lay with everyone and everything except himself and his son. He stood there indignantly, blaming the world, his head held high.

Unfortunately, he would not be the last "Sherman Tank" I'd come in contact with as a youth sports coach. These people often try to take control of even the league itself. They are the proverbial "rotten apples."

The clueless parents and their children perceive themselves to be perfect, never at fault. So when something goes awry, you can bet who's to blame. They're a coach's worst nightmare.

The clueless parents use phrases such as, "It's not my fault," and blame everyone else. Their children say, "It's not my fault," and their expression says, "Everyone's against me." These children are neither accepting nor accepted by their peers.

The keys these parents lack are communication and acceptance. Unfortunately for the poor coach, it's not presence that's missing.

The Compound Problem

How do you know if you are a clueless parent? If you haven't identified with one of the preceding personality types, then chances are you're "clueless" about your own shortcomings. To a certain degree, we are all "clueless" at some time, failing to see that the obvious fault lies with ourselves and placing the blame on others. I call this the "compound problem": not recognizing the fault is yours but putting the blame on someone else. This is how the one rotten apple spoils the bunch. To help you recognize which kind of parent you are and to break harmful patterns, review the personality types listed in this chapter.

6. The Accepting Parent, Imperfect but Real

Joyce played in midfield. She worked hard for the team, chased the ball, and tackled well. She helped out in defense when the other team was threatening her goal, and supported her strikers when they were going forward. She didn't do everything right, though. She made bad passes, missed easy shots, and lost the ball at crucial times. But she tried her best and had fun. The rest of the team liked her. Her parents cheered from the sidelines, congratulated her when she did something well, and encouraged her when she made an error. Her parents were aware of Joyce's and their own shortcomings and could laugh about them.

If you've identified with every category so far, chances are you can see yourself as others see you—imperfect but real—and you are an accepting parent.

The accepting parents use phrases such as, "That's OK, you'll do it next time, we all make mistakes." These parents are not afraid of making self-deprecating jokes and don't take themselves too seriously. Their children say things like, "I'll try it again, I just need practice, I can do it."

Their children are both accepting and accepted by their peers. They are fun to be around. Their parents use the four keys to success and, most important, they realize that imperfection is perfectly OK.

From the Doctor's Desk

Acceptance is the key to success. It nurtures healthy self-esteem, self-confidence, and knowledge of one's boundaries.

We all have unhealthy traits as well as commendable ones. The key is to maintain a balance and focus on the goal of kids' soccer: the child's physical, emotional, psychological, and moral development.

There are three simple steps for coaches to deal with parents who lose focus:

1. Affirm their good intentions.
2. Confront their actions.
3. Give alternative solutions.

For the Overachieving Parent

Sometimes the overachieving parent is the most difficult one to deal with, especially if you, the coach, feel he may be smarter, richer, or have more prestige within the community than you. But always remember, it's not *who* you are, but *what* you are that counts. You are the coach, someone who cares so much that you give up your free time. No one is better than you, especially those who think they are.

To the likes of Mrs. Bigwig: It's wonderful you're out here for your child. I know she means the world to you, just as she is important to me and to the team. (Affirm her good intentions.)

But don't you think that at times you put too much pressure on her? What if she doesn't make straight A's? Will she understand why you don't accept her? At times I see her shoulders sag instead of perk up when you say how great she is. Sometimes too much praise weighs a child down. I know that's not what you want. (Confront her actions and their consequences.)

How about the next time forget about how she does in school and the goals she scored last time and just compliment her on the effort she's giving and how proud you are of her. (Give alternative solutions.)

For the Unfulfilled Parent

It's probably the type of parent we can all readily empathize with—most of us have felt inferior at some point in our lives. As the old psychiatric proverb says, "The only sane person is the one who recognizes his insanity." So it goes for most of us.

To José: Your effort and involvement in helping your child is great. I just wish everyone could be so present and interested. (Affirmation.)

There is no doubt that you want the best for your child, but don't you think that your constant correcting and criticizing is making him uptight? He just doesn't seem to be enjoying the game. (Confrontation.)

Let's make a deal. You can teach him all you want at home, but during the game the only voice he should hear is mine. (Solutions.)

For the Clueless Parent

Handling these parents is a work of diplomacy that even Winston Churchill might have had a problem with. Make sure all your fellow coaches are in agreement with you. Against a tank, you need all the support you can get.

To Mr. Sherman: There is no doubt that you want the best for Reginald. (The affirmation.)

But do you notice how he gets upset when you correct him in front of his friends? What is all this "it's not his fault"? I agree that he is trying his best, but as *we* see it (at this point all your coaches nod) he needs more practice with you. (The confrontation.)

If the clueless parent remains clueless or becomes confrontational, you could try this: I'm sorry, Mr. Sherman. I do feel it's best you speak to the regional commissioner so he can place your son with a coach who can better absorb your advice.

This lets him know that you are humble and enables him to maintain his indignation with a way out. Unfortunately, someone like the Sherman Tank will realize his bluff has been called and retreat. But only temporarily. Until his next blitzkrieg.

Another solution is to say, "The other coaches and I recognize how dedicated you are to your child, but we think you are making things worse for your son. Can you watch how the other coaches and I encourage your son to help him without injuring him?"

8

Emotional Intelligence

The 8th Life Lesson:
Emotional Intelligence Is the Factor That Makes a
Difference

Being Intelligent Is Good,
But Having Common Sense Is Essential

The second impediment to using the four keys to success is our subconscious belief that our children's IQ is somehow connected with their eventual success or happiness. If anyone doubts this is true, listen the next time you're in a group of parents meeting for the first time. After the initial introductions, the first parents to speak up will be those who believe their child is "gifted," and if they can put a number on it, then there's just no stopping them. For whatever reason, society has conditioned us to believe that this IQ business makes all the difference. It doesn't.

Jailman Josh

"Dad, are we going to win again today?" asked Vinnie as his little brown eyes met mine.

"Winning isn't important," I replied. "It's how you play the game that counts." Not that I was counting or anything, but we were 3–0 for the season and about to play the only other undefeated team, the Hawks. I had never met the other coach but had heard that he was really good with kids. Though I hate to admit it, 4–0 sounded much better than 3–1, especially to us doctors where 4.0 and A+ mean everything. Of course I didn't let Vinnie or anyone else know that!

In my usual self-confident way, I absentmindedly wrung my hands, anxiously waiting to see the Hawks practice. I wanted to assess their potential, see if they had a chance to beat us. Then I noticed their coach. Gee, did he look familiar. His eyes met mine at that moment and he yelled over, "Vinnie?" No one calls me Vinnie anymore, I thought, I'm Vince. I still couldn't place him. Then he trotted toward me and awkwardly tripped over a rut on the pitch. In a flash I matched the clumsiness to the face. Josh, the misfit from my old grammar school. It couldn't be! I watched him trip again. Yup, it was Josh all right. I sighed with relief. As a kid, he struggled to get out of the dugout, let alone beat someone on the field.

Four and 0, Here We Go

Josh was one of those kids who could never do anything right. He was awkward, clumsy, and certainly no academic heavyweight. Even our teachers never expected much of Josh.

Despite all his shortcomings, though, I had always liked him. Once as I sat alone in the schoolyard, upset that my dog had just been hit by a car, it was Josh who ventured over to console me. "What's wrong, Vinnie?" he quietly asked. When I told him, he patted me on the back and said, "Hey, I'll share my dog with you."

Yeah, Josh was a nice kid. And he was reliable—you could set your watch by him. But like him or not, today he was going to be 3–1 while I would go to a perfect 4–0!

A Natural Knack

I watched Josh move methodically among his soccer players, encouraging and instructing them with a relaxed, jovial air. He was good with the kids, but it was clear to me that my team was more talented. The final score was 7–2, no contest. Yup, Josh was now 4–0 and Vince was standing in the corner with the funny hat. I watched as the parents and their children approached him after the game. It was astounding to me to see so many people regarding him with such respect and healthy familiarity. Then came the real surprise. A gleaming limousine pulled up and a man in a chauffeur's uniform walked over to Josh and said, "Mr. Smith, your car is ready, sir. May I carry the bags for you?" It turned out that "Jailman Josh" was in fact the president/CEO of a large toy company.

How did the dunce turn into the duke? He was at the lower end of his class academically, and in terms of physical prowess, a close second to the Hunchback of Notre Dame. I remember an old saying at college: "What does the class dunce ask ten years from now? Do you want fries with that?" Today, that adage was proven wrong. Josh as a lad had little intellectual and even less athletic ability. So what happened? Did he inherit the toy company? Nope. Was there something that no one saw, a type of intelligence not measured by the standardized IQ, SAT, GRE, and the 3R's and not measured by goals-per-game, assists, and national team selection? Is there a secret something that is an essential ingredient to success and happiness as Josh was showing? Is there something we should be teaching our children and learning ourselves, something that is not taught in the classroom or on the baseball diamond or in the batting cage? The answer is *yes,* and it's called "emotional intelligence."

The Secret Something

We've always known about emotional intelligence. Some people call it "common sense," and certain children and adults just seem to have it in abundance. Recent advances in brain science clearly show that IQ and aptitude achievement tests can be changed significantly if a child is properly taught. The same is true for athletics. Studies have shown that not only does practice and training increase a child's knowledge of the sport, but also causes changes in the brain neurons that enhance actual ability and potential. Neuroscience shows that we are not stuck with what we're born with, but that we can improve on our innate talents.

Daniel Goleman, in *Emotional Intelligence,* shows that IQ has little to do with whether a child will ultimately be successful, either professionally or emotionally. A study of eighty valedictorians, those with the highest grades in their graduating classes, showed that ten to twenty years later, they did no better than the average or below-average students in their classes. Another study showed that only 2.5 percent of people who graduated in the top 10 percent of their class went on to become millionaires. This figure is three times lower than was expected. But why?

It is an ability to learn and know from whom to learn that makes someone a success. In addition, an ability to get along and mediate with teammates contributes to longevity as a soccer player or any athlete. An ability to empathize, nurture, and manage relationships is one part of emotional intelligence. This emotional intelligence is inborn, *not taught*. Emotional intelligence, I feel, is the most important key to happiness with oneself and with one's relationships with others, and being in control of one's destiny. In other words, emotional intelligence is the common factor among leaders and respected figures.

Emotional intelligence has two parts: common sense about oneself and common sense about other people. Josh, for example, realized that he had a real talent for getting along with others, and didn't kid himself that he was something he wasn't. His parents didn't kid themselves either, but accepted that Josh might not have been the smartest in the class, but he was a sure contender for the nicest.

Josh and his parents had a solid level of self-knowledge. In soccer terms, they played within themselves. They didn't try to make Josh a rocket scientist when he would have crash landed, and didn't try to make him a major league star when he would have been a major league flop.

Josh had a natural gift. He was sensitive to others' feelings, took time to think of others, and tried to help them instead of only thinking of himself. By eagerly running over to me at the soccer game that day, by offering me his dog years ago, he demonstrated something even more than just common sense. He had compassion and empathy, the things that make a real friend. People like this are those that you always enjoy being around. They make you feel good about yourself, about life. They bring confidence just by their presence.

The coach with a warm smile and confident tone of voice imbues his players with that same warmth and confidence. It's contagious.

The Old Determination

Although part of emotional intelligence is inborn, there is an essential ingredient that makes it work: determination.

Some artists and writers I know have high levels of emotional intelligence and talent but never seem to be able to paint that final detail or write that last chapter. They lack the psychological muscle called determination, the ability to follow through, to be reliable and control passions and appetites. Josh, remember, was reliable enough "to set your watch by him." This stemmed from his parents' behavior. They always rewarded Josh's efforts with a smile and words of approval, so Josh always tried harder and harder.

It is the people who have the combination of both emotional intelligence and determination who rise to the top. Yes, you the parent, you the coach, can influence your child's focus or determination. As I'll discuss later, you do it by being consistent in praising effort rather than results.

Martha's Mom

Seven-year-old Martha kicked the ball away in anger and glared at Frankie, her fists tightly clenched. She was fuming. If looks could kill, Frankie would be in the back of a hearse right now. Thankfully, before Martha could throw a punch, her mother stepped in and I overheard her say, "Martha, you look much prettier with a smile on your face."

Martha replied through gritted teeth, "He pulled my hair."

Her mother wasn't listening. "Honey, you're always so kind and happy. Just go and join in the soccer practice like a good little girl." The color drained from Martha's face and she stomped away.

Later that practice session, I saw Frankie chase Martha across the field and roughly tackle her. I quickly pulled them apart and Frankie yelled, "She hit me with a rock for no reason!"

Martha smiled at me and said, "I didn't mean to hit him, Coach." From what I'd seen earlier, I knew Martha definitely had meant to hit him. She wanted revenge but when I confronted her, she just smiled and denied it.

Martha's mother had taught her what I call "emotional illiteracy." In other words, she had been taught not to read her own or other people's emotions. If a parent continues this, even a child with high emotional intelligence will eventually become emotionally illiterate. It's similar to taking a child with great mathematical ability and continuously telling him that 1 + 1 = 3. Eventually, the child will doubt his own perceptions and do one of three things:

1. Become frustrated and depressed.
2. Assume the same maladaptive behavior as the parent.
3. Ignore everything the parent says or does.

Teaching Emotional Intelligence

Parents can enhance a child's emotional intelligence by:

1. Helping the child identify his feelings or emotions.
2. Helping the child identify why he's experiencing that emotion.
3. Helping the child identify what can be done to change that emotion by resolving the underlying problem.

As a coach, you can help parents to learn these three points. As a parent, you must recognize your own emotions and help your child to do the same.

When Martha's mother saw her daughter's anger, she could have nurtured Martha's emotional intelligence by asking Martha how she was feeling.

Martha's response: "I'm going to hit him."

Asking her, "Are you angry?" identifies her obvious emotion.

"Yes," says Martha. Her feelings have been identified and validated by her mother.

Her mother should then ask, "Why are you so angry?" This helps the child to identify a reason with the feeling.

"Because he hurt me. He pulled my hair."

"Well, then, tell him you're angry and not to do it again or you'll tell the coach." This gives Martha a solution to her problem.

A Feeling Is Neither Good Nor Bad

It's very important for parents to recognize and understand their own emotions and to remember that there is nothing wrong with a feeling. A feeling such as anger or sadness is neither good nor bad. It is how we *act* on an emotion that can be good or bad.

How parents deal with their feelings and resolve their problems affects the emotional intelligence of their child. It determines whether a child grows up to be assertive or apprehensive, effective or ineffective at dealing with people and relationships. It determines how the child will eventually deal with adult relationships with friends, spouses, and coworkers.

Never lose the opportunity to help your child identify her emotions. If she doesn't recognize her feelings, she'll do as Martha did—adopt her mother's artificial behavior rather than deal with her feelings. This leads to a passive-aggressive nature which is anger acted out indirectly, allowing one to deny their anger or other feelings in a positive, constructive way.

For example, if a wife is angry with her husband but denies her anger, yet forgets to pick him up from the office in the pouring rain. Or a husband, angry with his wife, denies his feelings, yet also forgets to call her to say he'll be late home. Or a child borrows a ball from the coach he's angry at and then loses it.

The youth soccer field is an early opportunity to teach a child the lessons of how to recognize and deal with emotions. A child who learns these lessons will develop fulfilling, successful relationships as an adult.

 ## From the Doctor's Desk

Emotional intelligence is an inborn quality of awareness of one's own feelings as well as the feelings of others and the ability to draw upon this to guide one's behavior.

Emotional intelligence is not the same as character. Character is a set of values or virtues, a learned behavior one obtains through example and reinforcement.

Emotional intelligence has two central factors:

1. The me-factor: the ability to immediately access one's own feelings accurately and use them to affect your life in a positive way.
2. The people-factor: the ability to accurately gauge other people's feelings to guide one's own behavior, also known as "empathy."

People with strong people-factors often become successful salespeople, politicians, teachers, doctors, and religious leaders. People with a high emotional intelligence become:

1. The real leaders, captains of the team because they unite their teammates.
2. Helpers, the nurturers of relationships.
3. Peacemakers, the settlers of conflict.
4. Therapists, the analysts of social situations.

When we talk of intelligence quotient or IQ we should really change it to PQ, or "potential quotient." IQ is just one part of a child's natural inborn abilities. I believe there are seven parts to a child's real potential for success:

1. Mathematics, logic PQ (formerly part of IQ, intelligence quotient).
2. Verbal PQ, the second part of IQ.
3. Spatial relations PQ, artistic ability.
4. Kinesthetic PQ, athletic ability.

5. Musical PQ.
6. Intrapersonal (me-factor) PQ.
7. Interpersonal (people-factor) PQ.

Children with good emotional intelligence:

1. Know their emotions and are self-aware.
2. Can manage these emotions. (This can often be taught and/or greatly influenced by parents and coaches.)
3. Are capable of nurturing themselves and others; they're optimists.
4. Have empathy, the ability to know how another person feels, and share it.
5. Know how to handle relationships.

If you want to know who has emotional potential, remember, these are the people who can do the following:

1. Identify who is friends with whom.
2. Recognize and understand their emotions—happy, sad, angry—and the reasons for them.
3. Anticipate when help is needed, offering it before they are asked.
4. As children, they were usually not the most popular or the star, but were the ones who cared and were there.

Emotional intelligence, like the intelligence quotient or IQ, is inborn. However, it can be greatly enhanced by the parent, either positively or negatively. If you are now feeling overwhelmed, don't be. It is simple to do a good job. It just requires time, effort, and reading the rest of this book.

9

Development

The 9th Life Lesson:
Some Kids Can't Kick a Ball,
But Can Get a Kick Out of Life

Is My Child Brain-Damaged?

One afternoon in my rookie year coaching, I stood on the sidelines gazing out onto the soccer field. My son's team lined up in a defensive wall as the opposing team, the SoccerTease, prepared to take a free kick at the edge of our penalty area. The SoccerTease midfielder, Stefan, ran up as if to kick the ball, but instead dummied it and continued it. Another SoccerTease member back-heeled it over their left-winger, Miguel, who delicately kicked the ball over the wall. Stefan had now run around the wall, where he controlled the ball on his chest and volleyed it into the net. Wow!

It was a complicated, perfectly executed free kick. The other parents and I were in awe. Our smiles soon faded into frowns, however, as we looked at our own children still standing there wondering what happened. I wondered why my child couldn't achieve that sort of play. As I stood dumbfounded, I remembered my own abilities as a child with the soccer ball. I could shoot the ball so hard that when it hit the net the posts nearly collapsed. (The older we get, the better we were.) Now that I think of it, I never played soccer as a child.

So why wasn't my son normal like Stefan and Miguel? I could tell that the other parents had similar thoughts. Dr. Argon, a friend, wondered, "What's wrong with my child?" Mrs. Wong worried, "Was it cigarettes I smoked when I first conceived?"

"He is nothing like I was," muttered Mr. Finch.

Mr. Branus mumbled something like, "Is he brain-damaged?"

Since then, I've realized it is natural to always compare your child to those who appear the most talented, thinking that they're normal and your child isn't.

Comparisons

The most distressing times for parents are when they are comparing their child's achievement against those of another— whether it is SAT scores, IQ scores, or skills on the soccer field. The difference with school achievement tests is that the parents can hide, lie about, and justify the results. "Of course these tests are flawed." "I remember she had the flu that day." "These tests are meaningless." That is unless their child did well, then there is no shutting up these parents. On the soccer field, however, it is clear to everyone who is best and who's not. What we mean by best here, of course, only relates to talent or skill. Note, there is a difference between the two. Talent is an inherited ability. Skill is a learned activity. Just as there is a difference between IQ and achievement tests. IQ is an inherited ability. Achievement tests tell you how much your child has learned. Some children with average IQ have high achievement scores. This means you and your school are doing a good job. Recent advances in neurology show that those who use their brains do.

Tommy's Mom

"Pay attention!" Tommy's mom screamed at him from the sidelines as the Hawks' striker dribbled the ball past Tommy. Tom, like many seven-year-olds, was more interested in the puddles that littered the rain-soaked field than the ball. He loved walking in puddles, jumping up and down in puddles, or even rolling around in them. While Tommy's mind was on the waterlogged field, the Hawks swept past him and scored another goal. His mother glared at him then bellowed another tirade of abuse. "Why don't you wake up, Tommy? Come on, you're letting everyone down!"

A week earlier I had been to Tommy's birthday party with my son. His parents had a trophy cabinet full of awards that highlighted their own athletic accomplishments and I decided that Tommy must have "good genes" and would turn out to be an equally accomplished sportsman. But by the end of that rainy game it appeared his mother didn't share that view. Tommy stood close to her, but she, unconsciously I'm sure, turned her back on him and talked to the coach. The sad thing was her behavior was in sharp contrast to the other soccer parents, who eagerly chatted with their children and held them. I heard Tommy apologize to his mother then promise, "I'll eat my vegetables." His mother ignored him. He dropped his head, stared at the ground, shoulders slumped, and then tried to grasp her hand. His body language said it all. "My mom thinks I'm no good."

I'm sure his mother was not consciously aware of the message she was sending to her son by her tone of voice and body language, but it was clear to Tommy. She had confused his inattention with disobedience or inability, rather than recognizing it as a natural effect of his immature development. Also, even if Tommy was not so naturally talented, he had many other attributes to love. I hope my colleagues forgive me for this, but physicians and in particular neurologists are regarded as some of the brightest and most successful people. Most, I can assure you, either played on the so-called bench or dropped out of athletic activities because of a lack of talent. Remember Frankie and his dream?

Parental Reactions

As a parent your natural and conscious reaction may be to show your disappointment with your child in several unconscious ways:

1. To dictate rather than communicate with your child. Your tone of voice and body language is cold and stern.
2. To accentuate the negative. "You aren't paying attention. You don't try."
3. To avoid being closely associated with your child at the soccer field, thus provoking your child into attention-seeking behavior.

4. To not accept your child for who he or she is. "You're embarrassing me."

Children readily pick up these signals and translate them into, "Mommy and Daddy don't find me valuable." If you wonder if you are doing this to your child, ask some friends whom you trust. I am certain you can tell me the problems that other parents have with their children. If you have not noticed what other people are doing with their children, then read over the chapter on expectations again. Either the parents on your team are perfect parents or you need to train yourself to have a more emotional awareness. It is natural to act disappointed, but you need not act in a rejecting manner.

The Quick Fix

When their child is not meeting a parent's expectations, the parent often looks for a "quick fix," which will actually make the problem worse. The quick fix is often to tell your child everything he did wrong, followed by how great you did everything at his age and then by a command such as, "I'll get you lessons," or, "Better give you extra chores until you learn to kick straight." This mentality equals failure for your child and your relationship with him or her.

The chief reason parents reprimand their child is because they think people will think less of them if they do not correct or scold their child. This is sort of a face-saving technique. Unfortunately, it saves their face at the expense of their child.

A Child's Interpretation

Tommy knew exactly what his mother was saying. A child learns to respond to a parent's slightest change of voice, tone, or body language. Between five and twelve, children believe they are responsible for everything and their parents can hide behind words because children see what we say. From five to nine, children interpret a parent's reactions personally. They feel responsible.

Tommy interpreted his mom's frown and translated it into: 1. You don't love me, 2. You're ashamed of me, 3. I am responsible for my mom's unhappiness.

The reaction of the children on the field as they watch their parents' unhappy expressions on the sideline vary from, "Mom's crying, but Mom's mad," to "Dad doesn't like me," "Dad is upset about what I've done."

Tommy, I discovered, regressed to baby talk and childhood "peekaboo" games to make amends and to try to reconnect with his mother. This only increased her anxiety and her admonishments to, "Grow up, Tommy. Act your age." Ten-year-old Amy used delaying tactics. She complained of physical ailments whenever it was time to play soccer, or pretended she could not find her equipment. Delaying tactics are used when the child is saying, "Mom, Dad, I don't want to disappoint you anymore. I want to avoid situations in which I do." A third child, twelve-year-old José, used bad behavior as his way of saying, "You're right, I'm no good," or, "If you think I'm bad now, I'll show you what bad is all about." For children negative attention is better than none at all. This becomes very prevalent in teenagers. It is a way of both reacting and retaliating against the parents.

All these behaviors, of course, confirm the parents' initial perceptions and result in further rejection techniques. These include referring to the child as, "My husband's son," or, as one of my friends overheard his dad saying, when he was a child, "I don't know how he is so clumsy. Sometimes I wonder if he is really my kid." This friend had no interest in sports, but as he has told me he makes more money in one year than his dad did in his whole life. "Angry, still angry. What do you think?"

Where Do Outstanding Players Come From?

In coaching I have discovered that what distinguishes the average players from the outstanding players are the following six factors listed in the order of importance:

1. Living in a neighborhood with other children who also play soccer.
2. Having older siblings who play soccer.
3. Having a parent who spends a considerable amount of time teaching them soccer.
4. Positive experience with a previous coach.
5. Natural talent.
6. Maturation.

The first four have to do with learning the skills of soccer and can increase the child's inherent abilities.

The fifth and sixth points deal with inherited potential.

All parents must remember that the major ingredients children need to have a winning experience are parental support, discipline, consistency, and enthusiasm.

The Difference Between Maturity and Maturation

Maturity is the process of physical maturing of a child's body. It is often gene related. For example, children of Latin and Asian origin often reach full body maturity (muscle and bone growth) by age sixteen. African-American, Teutonic, English, Swedish, and German children, however, usually don't reach this maturation until they are eighteen to twenty-one. Those that mature earlier are stronger and quicker from ten to sixteen and can expect to appear as better players. Those that mature later soon catch up. I remember so well as a high school freshman being the only one at five foot ten to touch the rim. One of my friends, Tommy Breen, at five six, could barely touch my outstretched hand over my head. By senior year, Breen towered over me and over the basketball rim.

Development

Children's development is best understood when we see it in a practical sense; a helpless infant develops into a mobile toddler, then into an inquisitive dependent child, and finally into an independent, skillful adolescent. In medical terms, development can be defined as a systematic intraindividual change that is age-related. In other words, with each progressive year a child develops mental, physical, psychological, and moral capabilities that he did not have a year before. These capabilities are called developmental milestones.

At each stage of development, or developmental milestone, a child tends to assume that everyone thinks in the same way that he or she does. When a two-year-old grabs ice cream with his hands, his five-year-old sibling yells with confidence, "No, that is wrong." The seven-year-old certainly can't understand why his teenage brother wants to hold hands with a girl. The twelve-year-old looks at the seven-year-old and can't understand why he can't pay attention to the soccer coach and maintain his position on the field. A mother can't understand why her fifteen-year-old daughter can't keep her room clean. A father can't understand why his twelve-year-old son cannot remember to take out the garbage. All children cannot understand why Mom and Dad are so grouchy when they get home from a full day at work. A senior citizen can't understand why he didn't spend more time with his family.

Development is dependent upon the brain, auditory (hearing), visual, and sensory perceptual development of a child. If the child cannot hear, it is hard for him to follow instructions. If he cannot see well, it is hard for him to follow the path of a soccer ball. If his gyroscopes or coordination centers are out of line, he cannot tell that he is falling down or make adjustments to catch himself before he hits the ground. Likewise, if his brain isn't fully developed, it will be difficult for him to learn or remember.

The Knowing Brain

There is within our brain a part that acknowledges our environment. Some people who have had a stroke, for instance, lose recognition of the left side of their environment or either recognition of the entire left side of their body. When food is put in front of them they will only eat what is on the right side of the plate or they will shave the right side of the face despite being able to move both sides of their body.

The development of each sense leads to full motor maturation; the lack or partial loss of one of the senses leads to physical handicap and/or difficulties remembering, learning how to even kick a soccer ball.

The Senses

Hearing

People say, "My child is deaf. From two feet away I tell her to clean up her room and she cannot hear me, but let me answer the phone across the hall and she cannot only hear her friend's voice on the phone, but she can also hear what her friend's saying." However, some children really can't hear for significant developmental reasons.

The auditory hearing system includes both the external ear and auditory nerve endings in the brain and connections to the brain stem and the cortex or thinking brain that gives recognition of sounds received by the ear. This auditory system generally reaches maturity by the time a child is ten years old.

High-pitched sound comes into the external ear (1). It is transmitted to the middle ear (2) into a mechanical sound through the eardrum and ossicles; this mechanical sound is then transmitted into an electrical impulse in the inner ear (3) and transmitted by the auditory nerve to the brain stem (4). The brain stem (4) then sends the message in two directions. First to the limbic or instinct or emotional brain (5). Then to the brain cortex (6), called Wernikes area, where the sound is identified from many possible sounds as a siren. Before the electrical impulse goes to (6), it first is sent to the limbic or instinctive or emotional brain where a siren causes an alarm reaction, a scared

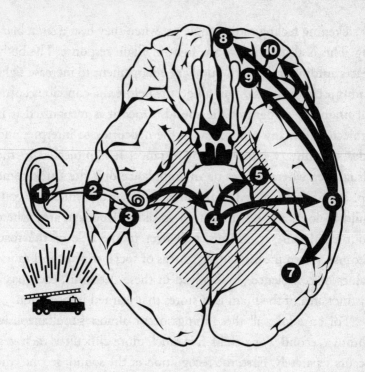

1. Ear
2. Ear Drum
3. Auditory Nerve
4. Brain Stem
5. Limbic Instinct Memory System (Gray Zone)
6. Wernikes Area (Sound Recognition)
7. Vision Recognition Memory
8. Executive (Action Planner)
9. Conscience
10. Social Control

or sickening feeling most people get when they hear a siren blaring. This is also known as the fight-or-flight response. The body reacts automatically with pupillary enlargement to increase sight and muscle readiness. This all occurs before the conscious cortical brain (6) recognizes the sound. Once it is recognized it is projected to many other areas of the neocortex to interpret and take a voluntary response. For instance, it is projected to the visual area where images of an ambulance or a fire truck come up. It is then projected to the intellectual areas, which tell your child to look around, then to a speaking language area where your child can say, "Mom, pull over to the side of the road because a siren means danger." Areas of social control and moral values or conscience are involved in these decisions; each has a distinct area of the brain that stores that learned information.

For an adult, all these things occur almost simultaneously, within a second. For a child, it is much more difficult as each step occurs separately. First, the recognition of the sound; second, the visual imagery; third, its significance. You have done this many times with your child. You say "bow-wow" and then show them a picture of a dog. In time, with the siren sound, they learn it means danger or an emergency and later, intellectually, they learn from you what they should do when they hear this, that is what their duties are. Generally, by two or three years of age sounds are identified and from two to five they are connected with visual imagery. If a child has been frightened by a dog or bitten, the instinct part of their memory is imprinted with a permanent stamp to immediately tell the child to fight or run away from dogs. From age five to adulthood our duties, our moral values, our intellectual connections go to separate parts of the brain.

In soccer, therefore, the sound of a crisp thud tells a child a soccer ball was kicked; a crack of a bat would tell her a baseball was hit, immediately the image of the sound is created. If a child has been hurt by a hit ball, she might instinctively guard her head when she hears "Fore" on a golf course. They have an instinctual brain reaction for self-protection. Then their intellectual areas take over, they say look where the ball is coming from, do your duty, and run to it or prepare yourself to defend the goal. It is important for parents and coaches to remember that before the age of ten a child's instinctual reaction cannot be overridden. This is illustrated, for example, in baseball when a child puts his foot in the bucket as soon as he sees the pitcher wind up, or in soccer when a goalkeeper automatically turns his head away when a ball is kicked at him.

I know this may sound complicated, but believe me it is much more complicated than you imagine. So, just imagine what a child must do to understand a compound sentence with several commands. It is a miracle we ever understand anything. From age one to seven there are additional problems. There is also a pathway I call the "zone-out" that allows us to block out anything we do not want to hear. This starts at five and maximizes in adolescence. Some women say that it maximizes in their husbands when they get married. This "zone-out" is the reason your child can't hear you from two feet away, but can hear her friend's voice on a telephone across the hall. Children younger than ten are easily distracted and confused if more than one voice is heard at a time. It may cause them great anxiety and confusion as well. See chapter on "Attention."

Vision

The visual pathways are similarly as complex as the auditory ones. A child under seven has two particular visual problems due to a lack of development: first the eyeball itself and second the lack of binary vision that tracks an object with both eyes.

The eyeball itself, and in particular the lens, is not fully developed at this young age and is initially farsighted, meaning it has difficulty seeing things up close.

Binary vision is needed to tell the brain how close or far away an object is from the child. It is all-important for eye-hand or eye-foot or eye-head coordination. Close one eye and try to time something thrown at you. Or better, hit it. It is very difficult.

For children five to seven and sometimes older it may be normal for them to have difficulty judging the velocity or direction of a ball, especially if it is hit at high speed. At this age, they often have difficulty dealing with a ball struck to one side of them, for both binary vision and coordination reasons.

Balance and Coordination

So far if you thought hearing and vision were complex, coordination and balance are even more complicated. Coordination depends not only on vision and hearing, but every other sense with the exception of smell and taste.

Two important factors regarding coordination and balance are:

1. Posture.
2. Center of gravity.

Postural development depends on all the senses being coordinated by the vestibular, cerebellar complex that integrates feelings coming from the legs, images from the eyes, and noise from the ears. Center of gravity is essential to the postural abilities and, again, varies in the level of development between ages seven and twelve. From ten to twelve and to adulthood the center of gravity is situated at the umbilical or belly-button region. A five-year-old's center of gravity, however, is well below the navel. The curvature of the spine is also a crucial factor in determining postural balance and, again, does not reach maturity until ten to twelve years of age. Children's coordination, however, cannot be fully understood without understanding the overall nervous system development.

Nervous System

It is easy to understand why your child can't jump on one foot at one age and then can do so a year later. It is maturation. However, why from eleven to fourteen years old does a child suddenly seems to regress, becoming clumsy as he goes through a growth spurt only to then become better than ever several months or a year later? The reason is nervous system development. This includes:

1. Nerve cell maturation.
2. Axonal and dendrite growth, and paving.
3. Myelination of the nervous system as a child grows and matures.

Full maturation of the nervous system can go on throughout our life. Recent neuroscience has proven that with proper stimulation a person can increase his IQ (mathematics and verbal), musical, artistic, and physical talents. The belief that we have a static number of brain cells and connections is no longer held as true.

Neurodevelopment is probably the most complex and essential of all of the body's developmental stages. As men-

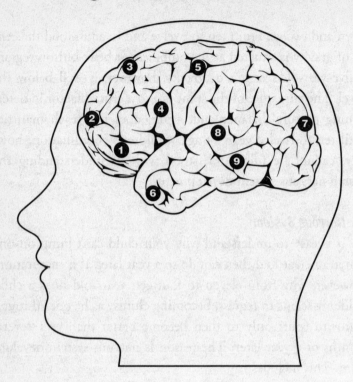

1. Attention—Concentration

2. Executive Function

3. Intelligence

4. Language Spoken

5. Motor Function

6. Memory—Emotional

7. Memory—Visual

8. Language Understanding

9. Voluntary Memory

tioned, there are three main parts to neural development. Maturation of the brain cells is generally completed by age four, though a slight addition of brain cells continues on for many years. The development of dendrites and axons form the "paths" each brain cell extends to connect with other cells; the myelins are the covering or pavement that allows the neural impulses to go more quickly from one place to another. The axon is like a dirt path: When myelin surrounds it, it becomes a highway.

The nerve cells are present first, then the number and types are determined by a complex gene and hormonal system.

The axons and dendrites then grow out to the nerve cells followed by myelin. This is more like a path or road being carved into a hillside than the pavement being laid down to allow neural impulses to travel between the cells. During growth spurts, between ten and fourteen, the development of myelin (the pavement) cannot keep up with the development of the axons (the path) resulting in a series of unpaved roads in which the neural impulses are unable to travel at a normal speed as they previously had. So a previously dexterous and skillful child becomes gangly and clumsy until the elongated roads of axons are fully paved and developed. The same follows for the visual, auditory, and coordination centers of the brain.

To give you some idea of how fast the brain develops, at birth the brain is 10 percent of its mature adult volume (reached at age twenty). By age seven the brain has already reached 90 percent of its total volume. Full myelination (paving) of the axon road does not occur until adulthood, which explains why teenagers have difficulty attending to obviously important matters. We also know that teenagers, in fact, have too many connections and that as the brain matures there is a "pruning of the pathways," which allows better emotional and physical control. This is most important in the emotional systems. It is the reason why teenagers are so emotional, so over-reactive, and have difficulty concentrating. It is *not* all hormonal.

Cognition

Cognition is dependent on the neocortex part of the brain. (See page 102.) Each section of the cortex has different functions and all are interconnected by axons and dendrites.

Cognition is our ability to reason and is dependent mainly on the frontal lobes of the brain, the last part of the brain to fully develop. With the development of the frontal lobes comes the maturation of the thinking brain. As all parts of development, it goes in stages. The first is called compartmentalization or egocentric thinking. Once the different sections of the neocortex can communicate, one can think abstractly. Until the age of ten most children are not fully capable of full abstractive thinking, only self-centered thinking because each section of the brain or neocortex is not interconnected yet. In other words, children of this age judge everything only in terms of how it affects them personally and do so concretely. There is then a gradual progression toward seeing things in relationship to others and realizing that "everyone is not the same as me." This explains why children under ten years of age cannot understand hypothetical propositions. "If it doesn't affect me, it doesn't exist," is their way of thinking. Teenagers who understand situations outside themselves and can abstractly think, however, often think, "If it doesn't affect me, why should I care?" (Children from five to ten learn best by concrete examples, by seeing, hearing, and doing.) Teenagers have to be taught and constantly reminded to be aware of the feelings of others. They must be shown that they are needed by giving them responsibility to fulfill a task. This is accomplished best through sports where they are part of a team whose members need one another.

E-MAIL

To best understand why children seem so inattentive, irresponsible, and, well, "just not as smart" as we adults, it is important to recognize how complicated the mind really is.

Cognition or learning has five components I call E-MAIL:

1. E: executive functioning.
2. M: memory.
3. A: attention.
4. I: intelligence.
5. L: language.

E: Executive Functioning

Executive functioning occurs in the frontal lobes and is the ability of a child to initiate activities on his own and is essential for goal-directed activity. When a child comes home and without prompting from a parent and gets his soccer ball to practice or sits down to study, that child is demonstrating mature executive functioning. This usually develops fully by the age of ten. (That does not mean they will use it.) It is the reason why children under ten need close parental guidance. Their attention is easily distracted and will often only do what is immediately available in front of them. For example, a six-year-old might watch dandelions grow on a soccer field rather than concentrate on the ball being kicked to him, or be unable to pull himself away from the TV unless forced to do so. It is therefore dangerous to a child's development to allow him unmonitored access to television, video games, and the Internet.

M: Memory

Memory, localized in the temporal lobe, develops very early and is part of the early thinking brain called the limbic emotional brain. The adult development of memory continues throughout life. If it is exercised, it will makc more connections and more memory can be stored and retrieved until senility, when cells begin to be lost and transmission interrupted. There are three essential elements of memory:

1. Recognition.
2. Storage.
3. Retrieval.

Memory is enhanced by all senses: hearing, sight, feeling, smell, and taste. With five- to seven-year-olds you need to use multiple commands to ensure recognition. In other words, a child this age is more likely to remember something if he hears it, sees it, and does it. So a coach or parent should explain how to trap or pass a soccer ball, then demonstrate it, and then have a child try it. This greatly enhances the chances that a child will recognize or inscribe the skills into his brain. In the American Youth Soccer Organization we call this "Say it, see it, do it."

Limbic Memory   Limbic memory is our most important

memory, as it deals with primitive lessons essential to our survival. It is most easily described through the discussion of pain or similar sensations such as thirst or hunger. These memories are the ones recognized, stored, and retrieved the most readily. In fact, it is a memory or instinct often forced upon us. It is also important that parents and coaches are aware that a painful experience on a soccer field, like an injury or a severe reprimand, is most likely to be recognized, stored, and retrieved by a child. This is why many young children fear heading a soccer ball and why physical abuse can be so detrimental and enduring at this age. Hypnosis can help one see the limbic memory by removing the inhibition of the frontal lobes. Until the frontal lobes or executive brain can override this limbic brain, children will follow their instincts and avoid experiences that have hurt them in the past or that they have seen hurt others.

How We Remember Once inscribed, the knowledge must be stored. Up to the age of five to seven recognition and inscription is slow and the brain connections have not fully developed with the storage areas and systems for retrieval of this learned information. By ten years of age, the system of recognition, storage, and retrieval is fairly well developed and this process of maturation continues through adulthood. It begins to deteriorate at the age of about forty-seven, when we begin to return to the so-called second childhood where our limbic brain takes over again.

A: Attention
Attention and concentration stem from a complex maturation of frontal lobes that allows a child to maintain a task when multiple other stimulants are present. From five to seven, chil-

dren are externally controlled. Self-direction, motivation, or executive function have not sufficiently developed. Children are therefore distracted by whatever is immediately before them. This, coupled with poor memory retrieval, means that children this age have trouble concentrating on intricate games. If there are other stimulants like cheering spectators, young children will quickly lose focus, forgetting their positions on the soccer field and simply chasing after the ball. They are mesmerized by the ball in the same way they are mesmerized by television. They follow the pied piper.

The Calm and Confused Systems Attention and concentration are essential for team effort. How do you get everyone to pay attention at once? Some are more distractible than others. Parents and coaches must be aware of special problems that the environment causes. I call this the calm, or closed, versus the confused, or open, systems.

Calm System—Practice A calm or closed system is typified by soccer practice or a parent teaching his child alone in the backyard. In such situations there is just one voice for the child to listen to, allowing him to concentrate on a single voice, the ball, and a few variables such as one or two other players and the goal. Children do well in the calm system environment, learn quickly, and develop fastest. The nervous system is not overloaded and they can process what you say, what they see, and what you do.

Confused System—Game The confused or open system is often the environment of the game itself where children can be overwhelmed by the larger environment and conflicting stimuli. Instead of a single voice of the coach or the parent, there are many coaches, parents, referees, and spectators. A child of five to seven is very often overwhelmed and easily distracted by the confused or open system. Here too much information comes in and cannot be processed fast enough to be understood by the child. Whatever is in front of them, they will react to. If it is a frog, the soccer ball is forgotten. Not until the age of about ten can a child maintain a clear focus on the game, but even teenagers and adults can be overwhelmed or distracted by large crowds at a game. It happens to the best in the Super Bowl or World Series or the World Soccer Cup. It is called stimulus overload.

It is important for parents and coaches to recognize the attention spans of their children. This will be discussed later in the chapter on attention. In general, the attention span of five- to seven-year-olds is five to ten minutes, often shorter. For a ten- to twelve-year-old, it's fifteen to thirty minutes. This is in a calm system. When their attention spans have been exhausted, it is important to reinforce instructions or refocus their minds through cheering.

I: Intelligence

Intelligence was once defined narrowly as the frontal-lobe capacity for verbal and mathematical comprehension. Now we know that intelligence includes emotional, athletic, musical, and artistic ability. It is not until the age of ten that a child's IQ (verbal and mathematical) becomes fairly stable and reliably tested. Recent studies have found that intelligence can be enhanced through continued intellectual pursuits, as can emotional, athletic, and artistic abilities. Yes, IQ is not static.

L: Language

Language includes two major elements: comprehension and

speech or expression. Full language development is not reached until age ten and continues until adulthood. See Chapter 3, "Communication."

From the Doctor's Desk

Developmental characteristics for sports participation can be summed up in the following table:

	Ages 3–5 years	Ages 6–9 years	Ages 10–12 years
Motor development	Limited coordination and balance. Center of balance and posture immature.	Balance becomes automatic. Center of balance near umbilicus. Posture becoming militarylike.	Balance automatic but can decrease in puberty. Center of balance is at umbilicus. Adult posture.
Vision	Farsighted, difficulty tracking speed and direction of a ball. Danger heading a ball.	Improved tracking of moving objects but still has difficulties and possible danger heading the ball.	Adult visual abilities.

	Ages 3–5 years	Ages 6–9 years	Ages 10–12 years
Learning skills	Attention span is short. Executive function poor. Needs constant direction, guidance, and repetition. Very easily distracted. Cooperation difficult. "I-centered."	Attention span still limited 1 to 5 minutes. Easily distracted, cooperation better. Difficulty with multiple instructions. Memory poor to fair. Ages 5–6: capable of hopping in place or walking on heels. Ages 6–7: stand on one foot for 10 seconds, eyes open. Ages 7–8: stand on one foot for 10 seconds with eyes closed. Hopping in place on one foot, 3 times.	Selective attention. Can concentrate on task at hand. Can follow multiple instructions. Memory fair to good. Ages 9–10: can maintain gait sideways. Ages 10–12: can balance on tiptoes with eyes closed for 15 seconds. Jump in the air, clapping heels; jump in the air and clap hands, 3 times.
Sport guidelines	Teach by giving verbal and visual instructions and have them perform the activity with you. Emphasize fun and avoid open systems and competition. Keep instruction time short—about 10 minutes with fun-filled activities in between. No heading of the ball.	Teach by verbal and visual demonstration. Keep rules simple. Keep instruction time to 20–30 minutes, then take a break. Can compete on a fun, minimally competitive level. Teach fundamental skills. Keep heading to a minimum.	Teaching can be verbal. Teach fundamental and advanced skills, with instruction time 30–60 minutes. Can compete without anger and excessive demands for effort. Heading the ball with caution.

10

Attention

I could see it in the Mustangs' eyes, each dancing with excitement and mischief. Every player was ready. They were my wild ponies ready to gallop to victory on the dusty plains of the soccer field. Even the weather was perfect. The dark clouds had retreated and the sun bathed the field in streaks of late fall sunshine. My seven- and eight-year-olds were in position and focused just as we had practiced. Everything was going just as I'd planned. Then the referee whistled for kickoff.

The soccer ball made a kaleidoscope of configurations as it landed in the midst of my wild ponies. In an instant something happened! The ball, I'm certain, induced a hypnotic trance, transforming them into anything but ever-ready soccer players. The fullbacks decided to take a siesta. Jimmy, the left back, even went as far as to lay down at the edge of our penalty area. Our goalkeeper, Micky, decided the painted white line that delineated the six-yard box was in fact a tightrope stretching across the Grand

Canyon, which he was now carefully tiptoeing across, his arms flapping about like a sparrow's wings to balance himself. Our midfielders decided it was just too hot and secured shade by pulling their shirts over their heads. I stared aghast at the sight. I was a psychiatrist, a neurologist, an accomplished athlete—if anyone knew how to handle kids, it was me. However, within ten minutes, my lungs exhausted, my throat hoarse from yelling instructions, I knew I had just met my Little Big Horn. I couldn't keep my wild horses awake, let alone corral them.

By this time, Habib, the Dynamites' coach, had a sore throat from all the orders he was yelling to his players. "Wake Up!" "Come on, defense!" "Andy, stand up!" It was only his exasperated demeanor that made me feel a little better. The harder and louder he shouted, the worse his players became.

What Happened?

High school, college, and professional players didn't just disintegrate at kickoff. Why did our players fall apart? What were Habib and I missing?

The obvious. Children ages five to twelve are not "mini-adults." Their ability to focus and concentrate for long periods is limited. The problem is, as adults, we fail to realize children's natural limitations due to their brain maturation. Adults' brains have well-defined pathways, like highways on a map, that make it easy to focus and get from one point to the next. Children, on the other hand, have thousands of pathways in their brains going from one point to another, making it very easy to get led off track. Their minds are like a maze. As they mature, the tracks that lead nowhere die off and the main routes survive.

Habib and I saw our players' problems as a lack of discipline, a lack of purpose. They were spoiled, overindulged kids who wouldn't listen. This of course led us to become angry. Our words and facial expressions, along with those of the angry parents standing on the touchlines, confused the kids even further.

Attention

Attention is the process by which we keep a goal in mind. To attain that goal in a soccer team, coaches give a set of steps or instructions. A child then has to concentrate on each instruction. For adults, it's a little like learning to dance. You know what the swing dance, for example, is supposed to look like but you have to deliberately go over each step again and again before it becomes automatic. When I learned to swing dance, I did OK in the lessons, but when the music started and dozens of other people began moving around me, I was lost. Eventually I just gave up and walked off the dance floor. That's what happens with kids. Can you imagine trying to concentrate when fifty adults are shouting different instructions from the touchlines?

We first have to recognize how long a child's attention span is, how long they are able to keep in mind their position on the field. Second, it's important to know how many instructions children can process before they become overwhelmed.

How Long Is a Child's Attention Span?

Attention spans vary according to age. The attention span of the average six-year-old on defense is about four minutes at the beginning of the game, and reduced by one minute for every twenty minutes they're on the field. Add heat, and take at least another minute off. That means that in the last ten minutes of the game, by the time the ball has been in play for one minute, their attention has gone and may be on anything that first catches their eye or ear.

A nine-year-old can concentrate well for ten to fifteen minutes, a twelve-year-old for twenty to twenty-five minutes. Then they must be refocused. Coaches and parents must learn how to refocus their children and the team. (Please see Chapter 18, in which I discuss cheering.) More important, however, they must recognize that what is occurring is not a lack of discipline or bad behavior but children's natural loss of attention.

The Short Circuit

Did you ever have one of those perfect practice sessions? The forwards, midfielders, and defenders, all working in synchrony, each child focused on your voice, following your every instruction. Every pass, every tackle, every shot on goal flows to perfection. No? Well, neither have I, but I came close once or twice.

On one particular Thursday, before a big Saturday game, I had a practice session that came as close to being flawless as I've ever experienced. And when the players arrived at the field that Saturday afternoon, I could see the steely determination in their eyes. Practice had gone so well, I was confident that each child was fully prepared, knew his or her position, and understood the tactics. The touchlines were crowded with parents and spectators. There was an air of confidence around the field.

Then the game started. I called out calmly to my forwards to make sure they didn't run offside. Then the opposing coach shouted something to his players. My assistant coach called out with another suggestion. Soon several parents followed suit, calling out to their children, urging them on with tips and suggestions. I called out to our midfielders to spread out—they were all bunched together in the middle of the field. But by this time I was shouting at the top of my voice to be heard above all the others. It seemed every parent and both coaches were yelling different instructions to the players. "Look up, man on, give-and-go, inside, clear it, hold it, look up!!!" Dozens of voices, dozens of instructions.

I noticed the faces of my defenders. Their eyes were glazed over, unable to process the barrage of information being hurled at them. They had completely forgotten where they were supposed to be positioned for a corner kick and were instead more interested in the sparrows fluttering behind the goal. Gone, too, were my words about spreading out in midfield. My midfielders and forwards seemed magnetically drawn to the ball. The game looked more like a rugby scrimmage than a soccer match. My ranting and raving had little effect. Chaos reigned and order fell. Everything I had coached during the previous weeks had disappeared. They were now straying out of position, everything we'd worked on was forgotten. It seemed the children had short-circuited.

I wasn't surprised. This happens frequently with five- to seven-year-old kids, often with eight- to ten-year-olds, and even sometimes with children as old as ten to twelve.

Why?

Children have limited capacity to concentrate. Their neural circuits are immature and are quickly saturated, and once this occurs all that is taught is forgotten. They cannot sit still in a classroom for fifty minutes any more than they can run a marathon—due to both limitations in physical prowess and ability to concentrate when more than one voice is making a suggestion. When more than one voice is making a suggestion or their voices become louder and filled with emotion, it only leads to further confusion in their children. They can only take so much. Look, and you'll see it in every game.

The Calm or Closed System

A library is a calm or closed system for adults. Adults can't concentrate when people are talking noisily, but can when it's quiet. Soccer practice is similarly a closed system for children. Their ability to concentrate has two limiting factors according to age:

1. Their ability to focus and remain attentive is limited by time.
2. Their capacity to deal with instruction is limited by the number of people giving instructions.

In practice, they are generally listening to just one voice, allowing each child to concentrate on one voice, the ball, one or two other players, and the goal.

The capacity for children five to seven to follow more than one instruction from one coach at a time is very limited. Add one more voice speaking simultaneously and their ability to concentrate decreases 20 percent to 40 percent. Add multiple voices and their abilities on the soccer field become seriously impaired.

Confused System

The game is the confused or open system. As discussed, the child becomes overloaded and so retreats into his own world that he can manage, whether it be focusing on the sparrows or chasing after the ball in any direction. Positions, strategy, all focus is lost. They cannot handle more than one thing at a time with all this noise and confusion going on around them.

This does not mean we shouldn't cheer. No, shouting, "Go Bears! Go!" applauding, and cheering is different than shouting, "Cross it early! Cover the near post! Pass it out wide!"

How to Keep the Team Focused and Your Sanity Intact

1. Keep it fun: smile, laugh, let your voice sound reassuring, let your body language tell them it's playtime. A high five and keeping your eyes at their level gives them the message that you're on their side.
2. Don't overload your child or your team with multiple commands. At best they can handle three instructions at once in a closed environment. Keep your game plan simple, so as to not short circuit them.
3. Children under twelve love repetitious movements—it keeps their circuits intact. Use drills to keep the goalkeeper and defenders focused when their team is attacking and the ball is at the other end of the field. Use drills to encourage forwards to drop back in support when their team is defending.
4. Most important is cheering. Have parents chant well-known

cheers such as "2-4-6-8, who do we appreciate!" Let the instructions be given only by the coaches.

5. Use a team "charge." When attention begins to wane and the entire team needs an energy boost, use cheering and chanting. "Who are we? The Mustangs!" "Do we ever give up? Never! Never! Never!" Always make cheers in threes.

Attention Deficit Disorder (ADD)

Nick, eleven, arrived as usual without the right equipment. This time he forgot his shin guards, last time he brought two left shoes. His mom was always embarrassed because no matter how hard she tried, Nick never seemed able to get organized. In games and practice, Nick really tried, but if for one moment the ball was not within his sight, he was distracted. Once, while everyone had his eyes on the ball, Nick, a forward, had his eye on an ever-growing white line in the sky. Amazingly, a group of players kicked the ball all around him without his noticing.

At halftime Nick did not recognize his mom's distress, nor mine, nor his teammates'. His lack of social recognition and hyperactivity often got him into trouble. After the second game, his dad just stopped coming. Yes, Nick suffered from ADD, characterized by an overall distractibility, poor organization, hyperactivity—especially during games—and poor social skills. The latter was due to an inability to recognize social cues such as an angry or concerned face. In fact, one of the special problems of ADD children is their inability to recognize emotional facial features, which would tell them they're in trouble. Once these children begin to feel bad about themselves, they will often act out and live up to everyone's negative opinion. These children need professional help and consistently loving parents who recognize their child's problems and are united in helping him deal with them.

We must always remember that there are seven factors to anyone's overall potential. Some ADD children are highly creative. Others who lack physical ability possess other talents, often high emotional IQ because of their recognition of how it feels not to be understood. It is up to us, the parents and coaches, to recognize a problem when it is small. We must be together as a team, Mom, Dad, and coach, to maximize a child's potential. Sometimes creative storytelling can change a child's view of himself. "The Turtle and the Hare" is one, "David and Goliath" another.

From the Doctor's Desk

Some children have real physical and intellectual problems that can hamper them for the rest of their lives if not treated.

1. Parents and coaches must admit there is a problem and obtain competent evaluation. Recognizing a problem when it is small prevents a large unsolvable problem later on.

2. Recognize that a child's potential does not depend on only physical, or mathematical, or verbal IQ. There are other types of potentials such as artistic, musical, and mechanical that if recognized and maximized can lead to increased self-confidence. A close friend's child, too awkward to play baseball or soccer, and too hyperactive in school, dropped out of

high school at sixteen years of age. At twenty, he is earning $90,000 a year as a computer programmer.

3. Parents and coaches must work with their children in a consistent and supportive way. Children who are hyperactive must be kept busy. "Shut up," "Sit down," does not work. Children without physical talent that becomes more apparent year after year should not be forced into sports. It may be counterproductive. Learn their real strengths and praise them. Just because you were a jock does not mean that your son or daughter must be one. Don't become part of the problem by forcing your child to fail. There is a difference between inability and lack of effort. Parents and coaches must recognize the difference.

4. Get a doctor's opinion. Too many children with epilepsy or asthma are kept out of sports unnecessarily. They can play if a doctor feels that it is OK, and most often it is.

Parents and coaches must remember:

1. Children aged five to eighteen have limited attention spans. You must be aware of this and that each child's attention span differs. Know your child's limits.

2. Children in a calm environment (practice) concentrate better and for longer periods than in a confused environment (the game).

3. It is most important that the parents and coaches are in focus and in unison—it will help the young players concentrate and have fun and will avoid confusion. Thirty-five percent of kids lose interest because the sense of confusion becomes too great to bear.

PART III

SOCCER IS SPELLED C-H-A-R-A-C-T-E-R

What Lies Behind Us and What Lies Before Us Are
Tiny Matters Compared to What Lies Within Us
—RALPH WALDO EMERSON

It's unanimous. No one argues it. What children need to learn most from soccer is how to develop character. Character, not talent, is your child's destiny.

When does a farmer first nurture his field? When does a teacher begin to teach the basics of math, reading, and writing? When should a parent plant the seeds of success in her child? Reason dictates that the answer to each is "at the earliest opportunity."

Soccer provides that opportunity.

It is the field on which to impart and nurture the seeds of character, conscience, and courage.

Remember, character determines our fate, but character is not determined *by* fate. You determine it by what you show or by what you fail to show.

11

Success

The 11th Life Lesson:
Know the Difference Between Success for an Adult
and Success for a Child

The first beams of early morning sun slipped between the trees circling Victory Park soccer field. I breathed in the cool, crisp air and a smile crept across my face. This is what life is all about, I thought, my son and my soccer team. Chuck, my assistant coach and a talented software developer, shuffled past without a word, as if he were in a trance. He hovered in the center circle, his eyes pensively pinned on the distant horizon.

"Chuck, what's up?" I asked him with a cheerful smile.

"Nothing," he mumbled without looking over. I'd known Chuck for twenty years. The uncharacteristic scowl on his face and the dark circles around his eyes told me something was most definitely up.

Digging deep into my psychiatrist's bag of jargon, I asked again. "Come on, what's wrong?" I wasn't expecting to hear what followed. Chuck was a diligent, hardworking executive.

For the last six months he'd spent every waking hour trying to secure a new deal for his firm, to which he had dedicated himself for nearly fifteen years. That week the project had fallen through. In less than five minutes, fifteen years of dedication and service evaporated. Chuck was let go. He'd suddenly found himself the fall guy rather than the new VP.

Chuck's son, Danny, assumed his usual position in central midfield as the players kicked off. Today the Bears were facing the league champions. Chuck watched quietly from the touchline, his mind clearly not on the game. Danny was in the thick of all the action. He dived into tackles when the opposition had possession and shouted for a pass whenever one of his teammates had the ball. Some of his tackles missed and many of his passes went astray. He even missed a couple of easy chances to score, but he was focused and having fun. What's more, he never gave up and kept trying his best, putting every ounce of effort and enthusiasm into the game right up until the final whistle. Despite his fervent endeavors, however, the Bears lost 4–2.

I watched as Danny ran over to his dad, his shirt soaked in sweat and his face glowing with the satisfaction of having given his all. "Hey, Dad, how'd you like the goal I scored?"

Chuck look at him solemnly. "It was for nothing. You lost." And with that, Danny's face dropped and he trudged off silently with his father.

Second Place Is No Place
—or—
Do or Die

There is not a parent I've met who doesn't want the best for his or her child. We all want our children to be a success. But have you ever asked yourself, "What is success for a child and how does it differ from that of an adult?"

If you asked Chuck, he'd tell you what happens when you don't succeed. For him and most adults, success is closing the deal, being the champion, the millionaire, the superstar. In other words, success is winning. Success is determined by results alone. Chuck and any professional soccer player will tell you, second place is no place.

A child's world, however, does not depend upon results, unless we, the parents, say it does. In fact, from a neurological standpoint, it is the repetition of continued effort that enhances brain cell maturation and the development of neural connections more than the experience of victory. Effort enhances a child's innate abilities, not winning.

Bill Shankly, a renowned Scottish soccer manager, once said, "Some people think football [soccer] is a matter of life and death . . . I can assure them it is much more serious than that."

The attitude that the game is everything and winning is everything, fostered by adult not child experiences, dooms a child to failure. The statistics of winning point to only one thing: Everyone is an eventual loser.

The Door to the Room of Success Swings on the Hinges of Determination

Success for children is measured in terms of effort and the ability to pick themselves up when they are down, not by the outcome of the game. It's measured by their ability to try, never to give up, to enjoy practice, to show determination. This is success for a child. And every child can be successful because every child is capable of trying his or her best.

Chuck had made a double mistake. First, he failed to recognize his son, Danny's, success in never giving up, despite losing the game. In fact, Danny was satisfied with himself because of the positive regard we all showed him during the game. His father, however, taught Danny the adult measure of success, that of "winning is the only thing, winning is everything." In so doing, he devalued the one factor that would truly make Danny a success: his determination. When a child continues to try, it means he's enjoying himself. This positive feeling makes the child want to repeat the actions that caused it, in this case, trying hard on the soccer field. The positive feelings derived from soccer develop into feelings of self-confidence that are transferred to other endeavors later in life.

The second mistake Chuck made was to lose sight of the fact that success is not determined solely by his job, but more by the warmth of his closest relationships, illustrated by the smile on his child's face and the devotion in his wife's embrace.

Adult misconceptions of success lead to five myths about winning:

1. Winning is final.
2. Losing is fatal.
3. There is more to be learned by winning than by losing.
4. Success is a destination.
5. Success equals happiness.

Myth One: Winning Is Final

For the Hotspurs' coach, Victor, winning is final. He was a successful businessman and now he would be nothing but the best soccer coach, manager of the championship team. What he forgot was that each time his team plays, the chance of winning is dependent upon the kids, the players in his team, not Victor himself.

Even if he does win, there is then next year to contend with. Only one team in any competition can wear the crown in any one year. No team manages to repeat the feat year after year. What pressure, what nonsense to believe that winning is final. Yet that is what many coaches and parents think. Worse is the parent who thinks his child will make it to the major leagues. The fact is 1 in 300,000 who play youth soccer will play in major league soccer, very poor odds. Winning is never final.

Unfortunately, so many parents, on their quest to make their child the best, harm their child's feelings of self-confidence in the process. Sometimes winning can be fatal.

Myth Two: Losing Is Fatal

In the fourth game of the 1998 NBA Championship, the Bulls were one point down with six seconds left on the clock. Michael Jordan drove toward the basket, tripped, and the ball was taken from him. He lay on the floor dejected and humiliated, although he had done this before. In fact, Jordan had missed the winning shot in the last seconds of the game 131 times. In the January 2000 issue of *Time* magazine he was named as one of the ten best athletes of the century.

What do Babe Ruth, Mark McGwire, and Mickey Mantle have in common? The highest percentages of strikeouts, especially with the bases loaded. Colonel Sanders of the renowned Kentucky Fried Chicken had his chicken recipe turned down more than a thousand times.

What all these successful people realized is that without trying, there could be nothing gained. Losing is always a possibility when one tries. But losing—if you've tried—is never fatal.

Unlike adults, children are resilient to defeat. Whereas adults will stew over mistakes and mishaps in a game, children's attention is always focused on the "here and now." This gives them the ability to keep trying without becoming discouraged—unless an adult convinces them otherwise.

Myth Three: There Is More to Be Learned by Winning Than by Losing

Coach Al was in charge of a very talented bunch of players, the Rangers. He demanded perfection from his young charges, and was hypercritical and unappreciative of his team's effort.

Brent's team, the Flames, however, had lost their first five games, but he recognized his team's effort regardless of the score. The players appreciated and respected Brent, who used their losses as teaching tools. They could go on the field the following week excited to be playing better and to show Brent that they wouldn't be making the same mistakes all over again. Their losses were not fatal but lessons to be learned. Although the Flames lost to the Rangers 3–2, the smiles on the faces of the Flames clearly showed which team had enjoyed themselves and learned a key life lesson: You can still learn from defeat. It's trying one's best and being appreciated for that effort, not being the best, that makes a winner in life. Determination stems from positive reinforcement of effort. We parents and coaches must never forget that.

The fact is winning does not build success. Effort, diligence, and discipline build success. It's *doing* one's best, not *being* the best, that counts. Every child, no matter what her talent, can learn to try.

Brent's team was less talented but they did go on to eventually win the league. Al's Rangers fell quickly from first place to middle of the pack. The following year, the true measure of success became clear. Chuck's players all returned for another season, while Al's players turned to other sports or dropped out altogether.

Since everyone will eventually lose, the most that can be learned from that experience is that it's OK to lose, just don't lose the lesson.

Myth Four: Success Is a Destination

The adult attitude that success is a place you end up is reinforced by popular media images. Lose thirty pounds and you're wearing a bikini and walking into the sunset with your perfect mate. Success is the Porsche in the driveway, even that cold beer in your hand. Success is that place. My idea of success was seeing my son's name with M.D. after it or my daughter's with professor before it.

Success is a process, part of a long journey that produces qualities that form your child into a well-rounded person, someone with honor, perseverance, integrity, and compassion. Success in youth soccer is achieved when your child picks up one of those values that will make him or her a better, more confident, more determined person.

I still remember a moment when I was a Little Leaguer and my dad rested his hand on my shoulder just after I'd just finished pitching the final inning. During that inning I'd thrown a pitch that conceded two runs and knocked my team from the playoffs. "It's just a game, Vinnie," he said to me. "What I'm proud of is that you had the stuff to finish the inning. You kept throwing that ball even though you knew you weren't going to win." True enough. I had passed the place called victory, but I kept on hiking.

Myth Five: Success Equals Happiness

Mark's son, Jay, was confident, a great soccer player, the team captain, and the league's highest scorer. He was voted MVP for our soccer team, but showed little enthusiasm when he collected the award. There was no smile on his face. However, his dad beamed. Everyone who knew Jay knew why. Jay wanted to be a guitarist in a rock band, but Mark refused to let him waste his time on such "junk" when he was such a natural athlete.

Would Jay have been happier if his dad had allowed him to follow his dream? Jay's achievement was an empty success.

Mark was an overachiever parent who thought he knew what was best for his son. And when Jay later dropped out of sports, he lost all support from his father. He retaliated, as many teenagers do, by becoming involved in gangs and drugs.

Remember, success is getting what you want. Happiness is liking what you get.

 From the Doctor's Desk

It Is Better to Have Tried and Lost, Than Not Tried and Succeeded

We can never be certain that things will always go right, but we can be certain that things will eventually go wrong. Adults and children have little trouble dealing with success, but it is how they deal with losing, with disappointment, that makes the difference in their lives. We cannot protect children from the world, we can only prepare them for it. Remember, winning doesn't breed success—it's effort, determination, and discipline that breed success.

Parents must understand:

1. Adversity is the mother of invention: it provides coaches and parents an opportunity to teach children how to deal with disappointment.
2. Winning does not build ultimate success.
3. Effort, diligence, discipline, determination (i.e., character) builds success.

If parents and coaches recognize only the score, then all children will at some point be losers. But if we recognize effort that leads to character development, then all children, regardless of talent, can be winners.

For when the One Great Scorer comes to mark against your name,
He writes—not that you won or lost—but how you played the Game.
—GRANTLAND RICE, SPORTSWRITER

12

Character Versus Talent

The 12th Life Lesson:
Know the Difference Between Character and Talent

If I asked you, could you define character? I asked two hundred coaches to define character. Fewer than 10 percent could readily give an answer. The majority said they would recognize someone who had it.

We must all ask ourselves, if we don't know how to play the game, can we teach it? The answer, of course, is simply no. If we attempt to do it, it's doubtful that we do a good job and more likely might do damage. The same is true with character development. If we don't have a clear concept can we do a good job? Probably not. This lack of a clear idea of character explains why so many people confuse talent with character.

The major problem I see in youth sports is this very confusion many coaches and parents have in distinguishing talent from character. Worse is the special privilege and adulation given a talented child, and the lack of appreciation shown by parents and coaches to those children who demonstrate good character. In fact, it often seems that parents and coaches who *do* recognize character are somehow out of line with modern attitudes. They are easy targets for the more "worldly" guys who will say and do anything to get ahead. The results of praising talent is evident when you open any newspaper. This is a problem many elite athletes get themselves into.

Talent

Peter was our best soccer player. With him, our team was invincible. Without him, we were vanquished. He reminded me of a player I had in my Little League team: a talented young boy who seemed to have a mitt on both hands. He was always taking, but forgot he needed an arm to give something back.

Peter was nicknamed "Peter the Poacher" because of his knack for "stealing" goals. When I first saw Peter, with all his talent and apparent self-confidence, I hate to admit I wished that my son had the same qualities, the same talent, the same self-assurance. What talent Peter had, what speed, what agility, what ball control. What a future, I thought, and how lucky his dad is!

Today we needed the Poacher to be at his best. Peter arrived a little late and was greeted by his teammates as if he were the cavalry arriving to save the day. As usual, Peter was a little aloof and warmed up on his own, dribbling the ball, practicing his shooting. The others in the team just watched him in awe. When the game started, Peter predictably collected the ball and dribbled straight toward the goal, never looking to pass the ball. He cut inside the penalty area, twisted past another defender, and made his hallmark move to score. But suddenly a defender, Christopher, swept past him, taking the ball from his feet like a practiced parent removing a toy from a child.

Five more times Peter dribbled the ball into the penalty area and shaped to score, only to have Christopher calmly tackle the ball away from him. Peter's usual resolute demeanor changed. The next time he dribbled into the area and Christopher came across challenging him, Peter deliberately elbowed Christopher in the ribs. The referee whistled for a foul and then Peter turned round and taunted Christopher with language that would have been out of place even in an adult locker room.

The next time Peter had the ball and Christopher approached, the Poacher fell over, his hands on his testicles, screaming loudly. The referee took one look at Peter feigning injury and waved play on. Peter's crocodile tears turned to rage. I can still see his pupils glaring through the slits of his eyes, his teeth clenched, his clenched fists red with fury. Nothing worked for him. Speed, agility, ball control—all his talent failed to get the better of Christopher. Then even cheating got him nowhere.

At the end of the game, Peter hadn't scored. In fact he hadn't touched the ball for most of the second half. He stormed off the field and never returned to play for us again, despite our persistent attempts to coax him back.

A boy I thought had the deck stacked in his favor, a boy I believed had the "right stuff" turned out to be just a self-centered, talented child used to getting his own way. His motto was, "When the going gets tough, quit." He lacked something, but that something was not talent. And to think I had wished for my son to be like him.

Character Is One's Destiny

What is character? How does character differ from talent?

All Hail Character

My dad, who was also my Little League coach when I was a kid, gave me the best illustration of the difference between talent and character. "Remember," he used to say, "talent will get you to first base, but it is character that will bring you home."

Vince Lombardi summed it up when he said, "When the going gets tough, the tough (those with character) get going."

All Hail Talent

Stephanie walked onto the field and it was as if Marilyn Monroe herself had just arrived. I stood back in astonishment and watched grown adults stand up and cheer. Her mom, somewhat of a stuffed shirt, seemed to glide right through the other parents ignoring all but those she felt were her equals. I felt a chill as she passed me and said demurely, "Doctor, how are you?" and then ignored Mrs. Sanchez standing next to me. Stephanie was just the same. The team seemed to take on another dimension when she walked in. I know in the United States there is no royalty but there was no doubt, because Stephanie was by far the best soccer player in the league, she was crown queen and only ten years old. Stephanie could be late, be lazy, and even be mean to the less talented girls and everyone ignored it. There was one set of rules for her and another for the team. Not unlike many of our major league athletes who are treated as royalty despite being human like me and you.

As I've said, one of the greatest problems I see in sports is the adulation given by parents and coaches to talented young athletes, while their negative traits are overlooked. One of the most astonishing stories I've heard to the contrary is that of John Nabor, five-time Olympic swimming gold medalist, who was disqualified from a race for failing to touch the side with his hand during a turn. Though he could undoubtedly have had the call overruled and been reinstated onto the U.S. Olympic team, he insisted on doing what was right, a decision that cost him the chance to defend his Olympic title. He wasn't sure, but thought that the judge may have been correct in her call. "If the rules are broken for the best," he said, "what does that teach the rest?"

Glorification or positive regard must be given in the same proportion to those who demonstrate character as to those who have talent. Those little athletes who have talent but no character must be taken to task as the referee did with Peter the Poacher. They must learn that it is not enough just to be talented, just to score goals, or just to be fast and strong. A child must be taught more.

Character Is More

Character is not just about doing what you have to do. It's about doing more, doing what is honest, what is fair, what is kind. It is about following the motivational speaker Michael Josephson's six pillars of character: trustworthiness, respect, responsibility, fairness, caring, and citizenship, which are also the foundation of AYSO's philosophy.

Know the Difference

It is important to understand the difference and the relationship between conscience, character, and courage.

Three mothers—Cathy, Millie, and Gayle—stood next to me while we watched the game between our Bears and the Hornets, as described in Chapter 1. They all witnessed Hank trick the referee into thinking he had made all the required substitutions by switching shirts so that the Bears' best player, Shawn, could play the whole game. They all witnessed our team maul the Hornets, and their goalkeeper, Armando, sink into despair. They all witnessed Hank's lack of respect for Armando's father, José, and, unfortunately, they all witnessed my cowardly words of congratulations to Hank at the end for a "great job."

As the second half wore on, even Cathy, Shawn's mom, said, "This is wrong. Hank is cheating by swapping shirts." Cathy was demonstrating conscience, an intrinsic knowledge of the difference between right and wrong.

Millie turned to me and said, "It's not fair. Hank completely demeaned José. That's disrespectful, irresponsible, and sets a bad example to the kids." Millie recognized some of the central elements of character: fairness, caring, respect, responsibility, and being a role model. Although Cathy and Millie recognized the wrong in Hank's actions, how he had fractured every pillar of character, neither told him (although neither did they act in as gutless a manner as I did by congratulating him).

Gayle, on the other hand, marched over to Hank, stood in front of him, and told him that what he was doing was wrong and the reasons why. It did little good because there were more gutless wonders like myself stroking Hank's ego than courageous people like Gayle. You can have character, you can have conscience, but without courage to demand that the principles of character and conscience be upheld, vices and the win-at-all-costs attitude will prevail and the only losers will be the kids.

How Does a Parent Do This?

1. Know your coach. If the coach is defensive or inaccessible, then go to the regional commissioner with your concerns.
2. If your coach is accessible, tell him directly and ask him to get feedback from other parents who have the same concerns.
3. Timing is very important. A telephone call or a practice is often the least emotional and stressful time for a coach and he or she can focus on your concerns without the distractions of a game.

13

Character: The What

The 13th Life Lesson:
Know the Six Pillars of Character

Let us become the change we seek in the world
—MOHANDAS GANDHI

Frances, a four-year-old with a blond ponytail, approached me after one training session with an earnest look on her face. "Coach, you're a doctor. What is that?"

I smiled and told her, "It's a person who cares for others."

Her little face frowned again. "Cares for what?"

"Illness," I said. "Disease. Like strokes or head injuries."

Like most kids at that age, she had all the questions. "And what is disease?" she asked.

I realized that you can't really explain what medicine is without first explaining about the disease it cures. So, too, it follows with character.

It is hard to understand clearly what character is until you see what happens without it.

Character has four essential elements, the last one of which can even be considered an entity unto itself:

1. Honesty
2. Respect
3. Responsibility
4. Courage

1. Honesty

Shawn was attacking the opponent's goal. He controlled a pass just inside the penalty area and pushed the ball forward to get a clear shot on goal. But a defender tackled him—fairly—stripping the ball away from him and clearing it upfield.

Hank angrily called Shawn over and told him that next time he was tackled inside the area, he should fall down and pretend to be hurt. That way the referee will think the defender fouled him and award a penalty.

Shawn listened in disbelief at first. "Isn't that cheating?" he asked his coach.

"If the referee doesn't see it, it's not really cheating," replied Hank with a sly wink.

Later that day, Shawn was caught stealing a candy bar from his teammate's bag. Hank called him over and asked him why he did it. "I thought if no one saw me, it was OK," Shawn eventually admitted.

Hank was so angry that he told him he'd be benched in the next game. Shawn was bewildered. After all, he was just following the lesson he'd been taught. Shawn, of course, being Hank's best player, was not benched, but I'm sure he would have been if he had been anyone else on the team.

God Help Me to Be Honest, Even When No One Is Looking

Honesty is the foundation of character. It must come from within, not from without. It is taught by example.

My son once told me that I'd just walked out of a store having forgotten to pay for the baseball cap I was wearing. I went to turn back when he said, "Dad, I'm sure they've overcharged you in the past. They won't miss it." I explained to him that it would be dishonest not to return it and that the clerk at the register, who probably earns only $5 an hour, might lose half his day's pay to make up for the shortfall.

"Besides," I said, "it feels good to do the right thing."

2. Respect

Todd was always the first boy in line for drinks at halftime and always the first in line for shooting practice, but nowhere to be seen when it came to taking the nets down or collecting balls after training.

Todd was known as a "ball hog." He was a selfish player. In every game, once he had the ball he refused to pass it to a teammate and would instead attempt to dribble it past the entire opposing team. When he had the ball, he was set only on getting a shot on goal, often to the detriment of his team.

To Todd, respect was only a means to an end. He showed respect to the referee and his coach only when it suited. Todd had not inherited this self-centeredness and lack of respect. His parents pushed and manipulated to get any advantage for their son. The behavior of Todd and his parents caused hostility within the team. Other players and parents were annoyed at the favoritism that seemed to be given Todd. He and his parents caused dissension and destroyed team spirit.

Respect—You Need to Give It, to Get It

A narrow definition of respect is honoring those in positions of responsibility, like policemen, judges, and doctors. But respect as a *value* means so much more. It is the acknowledgment of others' needs and desires. It promotes caring, consideration, and eventually team spirit and loyalty. From it emanates citizenship.

How does a parent teach a child to be respectful? The obvious answer is by setting an example. Parents must show their child respect by looking at them when they talk, and taking their concerns seriously. There are three habits one can adopt to start teaching a child to be respectful:

1. Get them in the habit of asking permission. "May I have . . . ?"
2. Encourage them to ask others if they need help.
3. Ensure they say thank you.

3. Responsibility

In soccer, as in life, responsibility means accepting, not denying, one's own accountability for conduct and obligations.

The Bears were defending a corner kick from the far side. Dennis, the right back, should have been standing on the near post to defend the corner, but he left his position. The kick came over and, sure enough, the ball swerved just inside the near post for a goal. Hank, furious, yelled at Dennis, who quickly shouted back, "Hey, Coach, it wasn't my fault. You know Tommy can't defend without help."

Tommy immediately retorted, "I don't need his help. He should have been on the post and now he's cost us a goal!" Hank, typically, responded by yelling at everyone. By not taking responsibility for his mistake, Dennis had shifted the blame to Tommy and eventually onto the whole team. Everyone was now to blame, and the team was riddled with dissension, the negative feeling that destroys fun and prevents growth and learning.

The next game I saw was in sharp contrast. Frankie, a fullback for the Stars, slid in to tackle the left-winger running toward him. But the winger was too quick for him and kicked the ball past Frankie and ran on to score a goal. A few minutes later, the same thing happened again. Frankie missed his tackle and the winger was past him and scored another goal. By the end of the game it had happened three times and the Stars had lost 3–2.

Frankie took responsibility for the loss. He apologized to his coach and his teammates and asked his coach to help him work on his tackling. He stayed after the game and practiced blocking the ball and making tackles.

Those Who Row the Boat Don't Have Time to Rock It

Children who take responsibility are the ones who will learn from their mistakes. Once children have accepted responsibility and acknowledged their mistakes, parents and coaches need to help them work on a solution rather than just reiterate what went wrong.

A sense of responsibility leads to self-discipline and diligence. It is essential to building character. Those who project their irresponsibility onto others cause a loss of trust and eventually destroy loyalty among the players and for the team.

How do you help a child be responsible? When a child complains that something went wrong, ask what part he feels was his responsibility. If he says none and you know a part was his fault, spell that out to him. For example, "You are a midfielder, so isn't part of your responsibility to assist the defense?" If it was not his responsibility, then agree and just tell him to let it go, it's just a game.

4. Courage

Hank broke the rules, encouraging his players to cheat and disrespect the referee and other players. But who could argue with his record of success? Three championships in four seasons. Somehow he always landed the best players—until the day that Frankie's mom, Gayle, stood up to him and said what had been on everybody's mind all season: Hank was a cheat. She contacted the regional commissioner and demanded he do something about it.

> *The Only Thing Necessary for the Triumph of Evil*
> *Is for Good Men to Do Nothing*
> —EDMUND BURKE

Courage is not standing up when everyone else does. Courage is standing up for one's values when everyone else is afraid to. It is the ability to do what has to be done, despite negative consequences. To Gayle, it meant standing up to a man who towered over her, a man capable of belittling anyone, a man who could take revenge on her son.

Without courage, all other values are voided. When one says nothing, one says a lot to children. It tells them that what is happening is OK or is not important enough to fight for. Courage is when "the tough get going."

 ## From the Doctor's Desk

What three things can a parent do to teach courage?

1. The soul of character is honesty and from it grows trust and trustworthiness.
2. The heart of character is respect; from it grows loyalty and citizenship.
3. The body of character is taking responsibility; from it grows diligence and discipline.
4. The will of character is courage; from it grows the strength of our nation and the protection of all the other principles of character.

14

Character: The How

The 14th Life Lesson:
It's Not What You Say, But What You Do That Counts—
Live So That When Your Children Think of
Integrity, They Think of You

Do As Dino

Despite the harsh competition that Hank always ignited among opposing coaches, and despite Hank's abrasive, often vindictive remarks, the Little Giants' coach, Doc Dino, chose to treat Hank with respect. The Giants' striker, Tom, received the ball at the edge of the six-yard box, with only the goalkeeper in front of him. With no defender between him and the goalkeeper when the ball was passed, Tom was in an offside position. Regardless, he volleyed the ball into the back of the net. The center referee and assistant referee didn't catch the infringement and awarded a goal.

Hank screamed abuse at the match officials as well as at young Tom and Dino. "He was offside—are you blind? Liars!

Liars, all of you!" Despite his great desire to beat the ever-arrogant Hank, Dino placed honesty above victory, the right thing above the winning thing, and calmly informed the referees that, yes, Tom was in an offside position when the ball was passed to him.

The referee thanked Dino and changed his call from a goal to the Giants to a free kick for the Bears. One of the Giants' parents on the touchline went berserk, screaming at Dino for telling the referee. Dino tried to explain to the dad that it was a good opportunity to show the kids that honesty was the best policy. "How many real opportunities do you get to do that?" Dino asked the enraged father.

The game ended 2–1 in favor of the Bears. But despite the score line, Dino was the winner. He had lost with honor.

Example, Example, Example

Character is taught by example. As adults, there is a danger in allowing our base instincts, our "vices," to overshadow our good character traits. Parents and coaches must recognize and curb the innate instinct to be self-serving and recognize that when dealing with children, the dog-eat-dog ethos of the outside world has to be left behind. Parents and coaches have to be exemplary in their behavior, because adult behavior is our legacy to our children.

If we are dishonest, our children will be dishonest; if we cut corners, they will learn that it is okay to cut class; if we deceive ourselves, they will deceive themselves.

Children Will Always Do As We Do, Not As We Say

Dino showed by his example that honesty and the truth were more important than merely winning. What we do, not what we say, teaches character to children. Through the example of Dino and his Little Giants, we find that honesty breeds trust, that discipline and diligence breeds responsibility, and that honor and integrity breed respect for parents, coaches, and referees. Most of all, Dino demonstrated courage to do what is right, despite the consequences.

Parents and coaches, you set an example for your children. Imbue a sense of humor into the children, let them see you laugh at yourself. They will develop an ability to laugh at themselves, not to take themselves too seriously, and will remember that this is just a game. Through that, they will learn the more important lessons of how to enjoy life.

It Is Difficult to Do One's Duty, When One Doesn't Know What It Is

As a parent, everything you do teaches by example. How you talk to your spouse or partner; how you treat strangers on the street; what you say about your neighbors when they aren't in the room; how you speak about employees or coworkers; how you talk about other drivers while on the road; whether you show up at piano recitals or your children's soccer games. All teach your children how they should behave in similar circumstances. Every minute that your children are around you, they are learning from you. If it's a baby-sitter or nanny your children are left with, it's the baby-sitter or nanny from whom they're learning.

The parents' job is to recognize and accept the responsibility for being the number-one moral role model for their children, and to act accordingly. Whatever you say or do, your actions are constantly demonstrating to your children your values, goals, and ethical standards, whether you want them to or not. The willingness to accept full responsibility for the ethical education of your children is crucial, and it is so important that parents not merely react to a child's behavior, but also take the time to explain to them why they should act in a certain way.

For parents and coaches to foster and teach character, it takes more than words, it takes example.

From the Doctor's Desk

The following are essential elements to teaching character:

1. Remember the purpose of soccer: It's a game for your child to have fun and learn.

2. Seize the opportunity. Every dilemma on the soccer field— be it a confrontation with another coach, player, or referee— is an opportunity to demonstrate and build the principles of character. Be responsible, be there on time, be respectful to the referees and the other team, demand that every parent, referee, and coach be an example to the kids.

3. Let children see what we do, not what we say. Soccer, like life, is taught by example.

4. Recognize your own competitive and self-serving urges.

Children will be children, but parents must be so much more.

5. Accept yourself and don't be afraid to laugh at your shortcomings. Your child will develop a happy and healthy self-image.
6. Live so that when your children think of fairness, courage, and integrity, they think of you.

15

Rules Versus Spirit

The 15th Life Lesson:
Rules Without the Spirit Are Like Soccer
Without the Ball

A big day, our Bears faced the first-placed Dynamites. Hank really had to beat this team, so I knew he'd be in rare form that morning. The Dynamites had, I'd heard, beaten every team they'd faced because of their forwards' "explosive" speed. The Bears had size, discipline, but little speed, and a knowledgeable coach in Hank, so today would be a real challenge. The regional commissioner would also be on the touchline to see this game. He was on to Hank for his shirt-switching plays and had already reprimanded him for encouraging overaggressive tackles from behind. He would be watching Hank closely this morning. I was softening on Hank. Actually, he was devoted, responsible, and loyal to soccer, but maybe cared about winning too much. But that I'm sure came from his marine upbringing and attitude. "A loss is not a win, no matter how you cut it," he'd say.

I arrived early at the field and saw the curious sight of a lone figure hovering at one end of the pitch. When I walked closer, I realized it was Hank. He was watering down the field in each penalty area, near the goals. How wonderful, I thought. Hank had faults, but he was dedicated. I continued on toward him. "Hi, Hank," I called out. "Getting the field ready for the game?"

Hank spun around in surprise. "Oh, hello Vince," he said, then hurried over to turn off the water. I watched him walk off awkwardly, almost as if I had caught him with his hand in the cookie jar.

Half an hour later, the field was lined with spectators, all buzzing with expectation. The referee whistled for the game to begin and immediately the Dynamites exploded down their left, racing past our defenders like a sports car passing a bus. Micky, the Dynamites' striker, made a lightning burst into the penalty area, the ball at his feet. He swept by our right back and was clean through on goal when the ball suddenly stopped dead in the mud. Momentum carried Micky forward, tripping over the ball, slipping, sliding, and finally sinking into the mud. The heavy, surefooted Bears' goalkeeper ran out to punt the ball up the field and out of danger.

I looked over at Hank. There was a self-congratulatory smirk on his face. Then my veil of naïveté lifted and I finally realized what Hank had been up to. By drenching the field, he had reduced the powder keg Dynamites to wet squibs, slipping, sliding, and sinking. I walked over to him and asked him directly if he had deliberately cheated by watering down the field to counter the Dynamites' speed. "I broke no rules," he retorted with a snicker. "If I did, show me where." The commissioner himself was at a loss for words.

The Bears went on to win the game 2–1 and Hank made no secret of his tactics. Richie, father of one of the Bears, thought it a "stroke of genius" and called it "gamesmanship." No rule was broken? What do you think?

Yes, there are rules and then there are the spirit of those rules, or why the rules were made. Basically, there are two kinds of rules: the ground rules and the rules of fair play.

Ground rules are just that, rules to give conformity or consistency to the game. For example, every field is marked out in the same way: penalty area, goal size, ball size, and so on. The rules of fair play, however, are there to protect players and to ensure equality. Laws on high kicking and dangerous tackles, for instance, protect children. Guidelines for playing children of similar age and talent levels assure the games will be competitive and give every team a chance to do their best.

Unfortunately, rules and regulations can't cover every possible eventuality. The rest is up to the players', coaches', and officials' innate sense of right and wrong, or "conscience." To hose down a field to give your team an undue advantage is clearly wrong, rule or no rule. It's common sense. The best way to judge what's right or wrong is to ask yourself if you'd think it fair if it were done to your team. If you think yes, then it's probably fair. If no, then chances are it's wrong. If you say, well I should have thought of it first, then my reply to you would be, "You need an ethical compass."

I've seen coaches teach kids to foul so that the referee doesn't notice. They call it smart soccer. Football coaches have their defensive backs wear gloves the same color as their opponents' shirts so the referees can't see them holding on. Basketball coaches teach their players to hit the shooter's elbow with their elbow, again so the referee can't see the foul. What they are teaching is beyond bad. You can't tell a child that it's wrong to steal then flaunt the rewards in front of him, or tell a child that stealing or cheating is OK, just as long as you're not caught. It infects a child's conscience and character. Remember, if you cut corners your children will learn to do likewise.

Conscience and Character Come from Within, Not from Without

True gamesmanship is training harder, teaching discipline, developing the courage to never give up, improving ball skills. Watering down a field to cause the faster team to lose possession in the mud and then letting your players think that this is OK, does double damage to kids. Other parents or coaches who witness such acts need to have the courage to stand up and stop it.

Sports Build Character

Many people believe that sports build character. They do not. Sports provide us with the opportunities and the challenges to build character. It is up to coaches and parents to use those opportunities and challenges to build good character. Hank had done the opposite and shown how to bend the rules for personal gain. The excuses for such behavior are always the same: "Everybody does it," "It's smart play," "It's gamesmanship," "It's ingenuity." The best excuse of all is, "If I don't do it, my team doesn't stand a chance!" Kids should learn it now, because later in life it'll be too late. All these excuses refer to cheating, to dishonesty.

In children's sport, as in any sport, there is *no victory without honor*, says Michael Josephson. Would you really feel that you had won if you broke or bent the rules? Would you feel that the other team had truly beaten you if they had to resort to cheating or breaking the spirit of the rules?

The End Justifies the Means

As we walked back to the car after the game, I asked my son Vinnie if he realized that Hank had cheated by watering down the field. "Yeah, Dad," he said. "I know it wasn't fair, but we did win." My son had learned that the end justifies the means. No wonder children think little of cheating on exams. Fifty-five percent say they do so regularly, and twenty-two percent say they steal from stores without remorse. Where did they learn such things? From any coach who thinks it's OK to bend or break the rules, for a start. From any parent who keeps quiet when it happens. By saying nothing, we say so much.

 From the Doctor's Desk

1. Bending the rules is bad.
2. Breaking the rules is worse.
3. Bending and breaking the rules and then justifying it is unethical.

If there is one principle all regional soccer commissioners should enforce, it is to reprimand anyone who directly or indirectly teaches cheating and that winning with dishonor is OK. Remember, there is no victory with dishonor.

16

Conscience

The 16th Life Lesson:
Know Right from Might

One of the most difficult questions I'm asked is *how* do you build conscience in a child? Just as with teaching character, it takes example, but it also takes the right words from a unified voice of referees, coaches, and parents. Unfortunately, 80 percent of books such as *Life Lessons from Soccer* are read by soccer parents, rarely by the referees who are enforcing the rules. So now is the time for parents to insist that all the referees and coaches read this chapter!

It was my third season as a coach of the Bears. Despite my good intentions and understanding of character development, my team hadn't won a game yet. My underlying pride was growing restless and beginning to show through my external "good guy" facade. I've said over and over again, have courage, build character, and you will win. How could I eke out a win while adhering to the principle that right must overcome might? With "might" being the other coaches who did everything to ensure victory. They stocked their teams with only the most talented players, taught questionable ethics, and let everyone know who had just won and who were the losers. Even the *Soccer Bulletin* used headlines like "More Bad News for the Bears"! The reports never mentioned the fact that I played kids no one else would give a chance to or reprimanded any of them who deliberately endangered an opposing player. How could I teach these children right from wrong when there was so much pressure just to win?

Frances woke me out of my daydreaming. "Coach, Billy keeps hitting me with the ball when I turn around. How do I tell him that it's wrong?"

I knew exactly what I wanted to tell her to do: Punch him in the nose. That'll teach him a life lesson. Instead I simply said, "Tell him to stop."

"I did," she replied. "And I even told him I'd give him half my candy bar if he'd stop." That's great, I thought. Reward him for doing the wrong thing. Soon Billy would learn he could start a protection racket by demanding a reward for not bullying.

"Tell him it's against the rules of this team," I told her finally. Frances walked away and I watched from a distance as she spoke to Billy. He nodded but when Frances turned away, he bounced the ball off the back of her head again.

How Do You Teach Right from Wrong?

Two minutes into the game and Denver, a nine-year-old talented midfielder, received a whistle for a free kick and then was shown a yellow card for a reckless and dangerous tackle on the Mustangs' player. Denver was infuriated at the decision and launched a verbal attack on the referee. The referee, without explaining why he had shown him the first yellow card, then awarded him a second caution and waved the red card at him. Oh, terrific, I thought. My best player was out and the team was down to ten players for the rest of the game. As Denver trudged off the field, I thought of Frances and her question to me before the game. How should I tell Tommy what he had done was wrong? How should the referee have told him?

1. Because if he doesn't obey the rules, he'll be punished.
2. Because if he does obey the rules, he'll be rewarded.

Well, neither had worked for Frances with Billy.

3. Because it is against the rules and the rules say it is wrong.

I thought every kid would have to carry a rule book with him and have a rule for every conceivable eventuality.

4. Because your teammates won't like you for making the sides uneven and losing the game.

I thought all these reasons sounded like it's wrong only based on whether it gets you in trouble or not. Maybe that's why so many coaches break or bend the rules—because they only act from these first four methods of explaining right from wrong.

The fifth, and best, reason:

5. Denver should not make a dangerous tackle because it could hurt someone and he wouldn't like someone to do it to him

and hurt him in the process. The rules are there to protect everyone.

Denver was angry, so I went over to him and put my arm around him. "Denver," I said. "Do you know why the referee threw you out of the game?"

Denver said sadly, "Because he's mean." I shook my head and used the fifth method above to explain to him why dangerous tackling is wrong. "Really," he said. "I didn't know that. I won't do it again."

I explained that the referee is there to protect everyone and make sure we all play fair so that nobody gets hurt. "At halftime, go over to the referee and say you're sorry, that you didn't realize why you got a yellow card and that you won't do it again." Denver did exactly that and the referee knelt down next to him and explained to him how proud he was of Denver's courage to come over and apologize.

Denver demonstrated character by accepting responsibility for his actions. He demonstrated conscience by realizing that he was wrong to place an opposing player in danger. He learned the most valuable lesson. He learned the difference between right and wrong. He learned the Golden Rule: Don't do something to someone else if you wouldn't like it done to you. The same follows with cheating, stealing candy bars, or wetting down the field.

If a child is constantly reminded why something is wrong, he'll eventually develop an ability to discern right from wrong and will always do what is right, what is fair. Wouldn't soccer and other sports benefit from everyone playing fairly, if everyone thought of the other guy first, someone else's child, the other coach?

From the Doctor's Desk

1. Conscience is knowing what is right and wrong.
2. Character is following that conscience.
3. Moral development is how one builds a conscience.

Having a conscience means understanding right from wrong. The concepts of right and wrong come from universal principles. It applies to all races and cultures, to the intelligent, the talented, the handicapped alike. Some of its accepted, universal principles are you do not steal, you do not hurt others, you do not kill. These are held true by all reasonable people. From these concepts of right and wrong come duties to protect those principles. Remember, children learn right from wrong, they do not inherit it, as they do not inherit character.

Without moral development, conscience, or understanding right from wrong, our society would fall into chaos. Imagine what it would be like if everyone thought it was acceptable to run a red light, steal from the grocery store, or cheat on an exam.

If cheating or bending the rules was permitted, what would it do to the teams and coaches who abide by what is fair and right? Simple: It punishes those who don't cheat.

Generally there are six levels that can be used to develop a child's sense of right and wrong, six levels of moral development. They begin at home but can be developed, confused, or destroyed on the soccer field by parents and coaches who act with prejudice against other players, parents, or coaches.

The six levels are:

1. Punishment: Is often used first with children at two and three years of age.
2. Rewards: Is also begun at about the same age.
3. Rules: At five and six years old, kids begin learning rules that give them a sense of what is permitted and what is not. They no longer rely on punishment and reward.
4. Peer pressure: At seven or eight years of age, peer pressure starts developing their sense of right and wrong.
5. Do to others: At about the same time, a higher level of moral development occurs when they understand that if they would not like something done to them, they shouldn't do it to others.
6. Inherent sense: Later, children develop an inherent sense of what is right, what is fair, and what is one's duty as a general concept if they are taught "do to others."

Parents and coaches must teach morality at the highest level appropriate to the child's age. They may in fact understand intrinsically what is right and wrong, but unfortunately do not know how to bring a child to that level of development. They often use the same principles of punishment and reward used for two- and three-year-olds to instill morality into older children able to understand higher levels of moral development. Hence, some children grow up believing that if they don't get caught, they've done nothing wrong.

If conscience or moral development is taught at level five—do to others as you would have them do to you—children will progress from there to level six, developing an inherent sense of right and wrong. It is not enough for coaches, parents, and referees to simply say, "That's what the rules say." Conscience extends beyond rules and encompasses the "spirit" of the game.

Level five sums up the spirit of the rules and should be the bench mark for all teachers of children. The sixth level of moral development will occur naturally.

Parents should avoid the coaches who themselves have never developed beyond the reward and punishment levels.

PART IV

HOW TO CREATE A HARMONIOUS GAME

Spend Less Time Concerned with Who Is Right and More Time Deciding What Is Right

Some things are not taught in school. They are learned from parents and through life's experiences. This section deals with how parents and coaches can create an environment that is safe, where disrespectful, bullying, or sarcastic behavior is not permitted. A safe environment is a fertile one.

Harmony requires parents, coaches, and referees to play the same tune.

"All for one and one for all."

17

Harmony

The 17th Life Lesson:
A Harmonious Environment
Gives a Child a Fertile Place to Grow

"Hey, Dad," my eight-year-old son, Micky, asked as we walked past a soccer game in progress. "What is heaven?" Before I could think of an answer, he asked, "What is hell?" Just as I began to respond there was a chatter of excitement on the field.

"What the *%@# were you looking at, referee??!!" the coach of the Blue Bonnets bellowed as he frantically rushed onto the field with his fists clenched tightly. The crowd fell silent. Anger, hatred, and venom flew from the coach's mouth. Red-faced, he screamed at the referee, "Are you blind or just stupid?! How could he possibly be onside?! He was a mile offside!" Spit sprayed from his mouth like a rabid dog. Sweat poured from the trembling referee. The Blue Bonnets' coach hovered over the referee like a snarling tiger over its prey.

I held my son's hand. It had turned cold. His face was pale at the sight of this horrible spectacle. "Micky," I said. "That is hell."

The referee swallowed hard and stammered, "I . . . I whistled him offside."

The coach's face went blank. "But you waved play on."

The young referee looked puzzled. "I did? I'm sorry, I get confused. This is only the second game I've refereed." Everyone in the crowd felt for this young man who had been so humiliated by the outraged coach. I looked up at the scoreboard. The score was 4–0 in the last minute of the game. Either way, the goal wouldn't have meant much.

The coach seemed to undergo a sudden metamorphosis as he looked down and first noticed his fists clenched tightly. He unclenched them and put his arm around the young referee and said, "I'm sorry." He then turned to the bleachers and asked everyone in the crowd to forgive his unwarranted outburst. A sense of relief returned to the faces of every parent and child. The chant of "Go Blue Bonnets" rang out. Harmony had returned.

"That is heaven, Micky," I said to my son. He looked up at me. He understood.

Heaven and Hell

We, the parents, coaches, and referees are in control and we can make soccer a heaven or a hell. Anger, tantrums, expletives, disrespect, and demeaning remarks are the fire of hell on the soccer field. Harmony and sportsmanship—kindness, sensitivity, respect, forgiveness, and the ability to say "I'm sorry, I was wrong"—are the white clouds of heaven. The skip to the step, the glide to a child's stride is heaven. You can see it, you can hear it in the laughter and chatter, a choir of cheers. It's soccer at its best.

Managers, coaches, and referees are primarily responsible

for establishing harmony on the field. But each parent and child also plays an integral part. Harmony is like an orchestra—it takes more than one individual to make it work. Like an orchestra, each individual must be in tune with the others.

The elements of a team in harmony are respect and loyalty, qualities that are conducted by the batons of courage and control—courage to stand up for respect and loyalty and control over chaos, the opposite of harmony. Discord is the boot of the bullies on the team, the "too good for you" children and parents, the so-called "elitist," and the parents and coaches with unrealistic expectations who come to the field not for their child's good but for their own glory. These are parents who try to live through their children and make them responsible for their own unfulfilled ambitions.

Fostering harmony is no easy job and can be impossible if these leaders are not aware of the responsibilities they have. It sounds complicated, doesn't it? But it's not. It only takes common sense and a sign in the locker room to continually remind the leaders of the team what harmony stems from. "Respect, respect, respect. We are all equal and valuable in God's eyes."

Chaos

Charlie was the chubby, awkward child that every team seems to have. He was more interested in the tasty snacks after the game than in the taste of excitement on the field. He was nicknamed Chuck and too often called Chubby or Fatso by his so-called friends. Tim was the striker, the prolific goal scorer and, as his father often reminded me, "Without Tim we have no team." Every soccer coach has had a Tim in his lineup, with an overbearing parent who personifies the adage "You are only a child once, but you can be immature all your life."

"Hey, Fatso, you're the goalie!" Tim yelled at Charlie at the start of one game. Charlie lumbered up between the posts. Tim called out again. "Remember to save the ball, not eat it. It's not a meatball." Their teammates giggled and started to join in. "Yeah, Chubby, save the meatball." I took a quick glance around and saw two of the coaches smiling. One was Tim's dad, taking great delight in the remarks. I looked back at Charlie. His posture said it all. He was dejected, rejected, and unlikely to return for another season unless his parents dragged him there kicking and screaming.

As Charlie stood nervously between the posts, the players on the other team snickered. Their striker said, "Try to eat this," and kicked the soccer ball as hard as he could. The only sound was of ball on wood as it rattled against the cross bar and bounced into the net. Everyone, including me, who was also a coward, remained silent and this mean, humiliating behavior went unpunished.

There was no harmony, only chaos, and obviously no respect. But there was a definite message being sent by the leaders—the referee, the coaches, and the very silent parents. It's OK to humiliate, to taunt, or to pick on someone, especially someone who appears to be a little different, a little weaker than the rest. The behavior is called bullying and not tolerated in today's society. So why should it be tolerated on, of all things, a soccer field? Because even the most righteous of us don't know how to confront it, and if we do, we can be fearful that they might turn on us next!

After the game, three parents came up to me complaining about the way Charlie had been humiliated. Charlie's mother merely escorted him to the snack stand, a sad solution, I thought.

The Power of One: "It's Called Courage"

By the following season, my third in soccer, I was less shocked by the behavior of these parents and children. Charlie did in fact return, dragged by his insistent father. At the first practice session of the new season, I kicked the ball gently to each player in turn so he could get used to the ball again. Tim and his ever-vocal, head-heavy father had already announced that Tim would play "no. 9," traditionally the striker's jersey. Charlie's dad asked if his son could play goalkeeper again and I gave him a chance. However, when I kicked the ball to him, he dived and missed it. It bobbled toward the net but Charlie finally got a grip on it and saved it before it crossed the line.

Tim shouted out, "Hey, Fatso, if that was a meatball you would have caught it!" The others laughed and a few more "Fatsos" echoed around the field. Poor Charlie looked mortified. I finally mounted the courage and walked with determination to the penalty area. My posture and my tone sent a clear message. I was upset, very upset. "Did I hear someone say something mean about one of my players? Did I hear some of you laugh at one of your own teammates? No one on this team laughs at one of his teammates!" My voice was firm.

Little Sean, our left-back, spoke up. "I thought it was mean, too, Coach." I quickly backed up the little lad. "When one of us is down, or makes a mistake, we must pick him back up and encourage him." I turned to Charlie and patted him on the back. "Good try, Charlie. You stopped it going over the line. You never gave up."

I glanced at Tim and said firmly. "The next time I hear a negative comment, that person will be off the team. Understood?" I gazed around at my players. To my surprise, there was no terror in their eyes. For now there was no need to fear the bullies. Harmony had been restored. They had been reminded that we must respect, support, and be loyal to one another to really call ourselves a team.

Bullies may seem popular, but their popularity is established through fear and intimidation. When they fall, no one wants to pick them up. Which is exactly why they never try to pick anyone else up. Any team governed by disrespect and disloyalty is a bully's ground, and doomed, as are those leaders who allow it to prevail.

Tim's father asked the regional commissioner to switch his son to another team. Though I needed Tim on the field I truly did not need their attitude.

Rejection

Looking back to our childhood none of us can forget when one of our own peers, a so-called friend, hurt us. Perhaps the other girls excluded you from playing dolls, or in high school the "in crowd" left you out of the birthday party. For me it was the time I was six years old playing hide-and-seek with my friends. I found a great place to hide. As time went by I thought maybe it was "too good." I slowly crept down from the tree to find them. They had all disappeared. My first thought was maybe a Martian had come and gobbled them up. When I arrived at "home-base" it, too, was empty. Then, way down the block I saw them. I could still feel the emptiness. They couldn't find me because they forgot me. These feelings of rejection are some of the strongest negative memories, because they originate from our deepest fears as a child stored in our limbic memory. They are those of being abandoned, of being alone and unprotected.

When we allow children to be belittled, to be left out, we are creating an environment that will harm rather than help their confidence.

I know you're asking, why do adults allow this to happen? Haven't they been hurt? Don't they know better?

What Comes Natural?
Instincts

Harmony, treating everyone kindly, is not a natural instinct. Instincts are primarily for survival, control, or power. A child's instinct is to judge other children on who is "in," who is "cool," and who is not. For adults, it's more a case of who's "on top."

When the coaches laughed at Tim's jokes about Charlie, and failed to stop it, the message to the children was, it's OK to behave like that. This kind of message increases the likelihood of further destructive behavior by the "in crowd." The result for the other children is fear and an undermining of the principles of respect, caring, and team loyalty.

Coaches must be in charge, not only of making certain everyone is on time, practicing and learning new skills. The coaches' most important job is to ensure each child a fertile soccer field to grow as a person, protected from the bullies who can make it a thorny field.

Coaches must remember to live up to their name:

C: Care for each child.

O: Create objectives that build self-esteem and treat all children equally.

A: Attitude is always positive.

C: Have courage to do what is right for the kids at all times.

H: Humor makes soccer fun so children want to return.

Larson

Tom Larson, Colin's dad, introduced himself to Denver's dad, Brent. "Hi! My name is Tom," he said, gripping Brent's hand firmly, to the point that Brent, a big guy, winced. "Looks like they're having fun. Which boy is yours?" Brent pointed to his son, Denver, who stood a full head taller than Tom's son, Colin. Denver was as quick and talented as he was big. Now feeling a little insecure, Tom started what I call, "the who's on top game." "Where do you live?" he asked. Before Brent could answer, Tom blurted, "I live in Beverly Hills. Hold on, my cell phone is vibrating. It must be my client, Michael. You know, 'Air Jordan.'" Brent just smiled. He was secure enough not to play the game, despite being the finest hand surgeon in the state.

Grown-Up Children

Yes, adults may be no more than grown-up children. It's not who's in or who's out, it's who's down and who's on top; it's status. Some people can grow up but never mature. It is especially prevalent in those people whose values depend on who they hang out with (the name-droppers) or those who are insecure in what they do (CEO, attorney, director), whose accomplishments have not yet helped them grow secure. We all have a certain degree of these insecurities and there is rarely anyone who hasn't been left out. We adults must remember how bad it felt.

Every parent and especially every coach must recognize these prime responsibilities to protect our children from harm, both physical and emotional. Emotional pain—being rejected and being made fun of—can leave scars as much as a cut.

Every coach and parent must remember how she felt when left out or picked on and remember it might seem trivial to you, but if it repeatedly occurs it can hurt a child for many years. Insist on a harmonious environment. Be HONEST:

H: Honor and respect each child regardless of his talent.

O: Organize your practices and games so every athlete on your team has an opportunity to develop and maintain positive feelings of self-worth.

N: Need to understand that players want to enjoy attending practice games. If they are not having fun and learning, they will lose interest and not return.

E: Encouragement is needed, not only when your kids do well, but especially when they are discouraged. Being honest with your encouragement means a lot to players and children.

S: Sensitivity to parents, coaches, children, and others is important. All look to you for direction and fairness and someone who's available to hear their concerns.

T: Try to be an example of caring, character, and courage. Stand up for what is right, not who is right. A good coach is an example. A great coach is an inspiration.

Basic Instincts

These "basic" instincts are within us all and can cause destructive behavior and an atmosphere of discord on the soccer field. What characterizes civilized people is their ability to suppress the instinct to dominate another person, usually the weak, the small, those less fortunate. This in turn creates harmony, a nice place to bring up children.

Character and moral development are dependent on controlling these instincts. Discord causes children to be fearful and develop vices such as selfishness, bullying, disloyalty, and dishonesty. Harmony nurtures growth in children. It builds character and values, which are keys to children becoming successful.

 From the Doctor's Desk

1. Harmony is the "team spirit" and "team unity."
2. It differs from character and moral development in that it is the synchrony of coach, referee, and parent working together to create an overall harmonious environment. It depends on character and conscience and can never exist without them.
3. That spirit and unity is instilled by the leaders but depends on the cooperation of every parent and player.
4. Each leader, coach, and regional commissioner must recognize discord and have the courage to confront it. The principles of doing this are simple:

   • Give respect and demand respect from every child, parent, and authority figure.

- Give loyalty and demand loyalty from every player.
- Remind each child and parent that he must be "all for one and one for all."

Doing this enhances a child's innate emotional potential, his ability to understand himself and be sensitive to others. It is the bread and butter of making friends, being a friend, and, ultimately, being a success.

18

Cheering

The 18th Life Lesson:
Cheering Is More Than Noise; It's the
Heartbeat of Harmony

Cheering is not just noise. Appropriate cheering causes a physical response that heightens a child's abilities. Appropriate cheering for children has a rhythmic and very repetitive quality that helps to energize and focus youngsters.

The problem is parents tend to cheer only when the child is winning, not when children need it the most, when they are losing or tired. The reason for this is adult logic: How can you cheer when your team is down? If one understands what cheering does for a child, it becomes illogical not to cheer when he's down. Besides, as we've discussed, winning to a child is not nearly as important as having fun.

Mr. Carter yawned and Mrs. O'Brien frowned. "What's happening here, what is this game?" her expression seemed to say. Mr. Torez tapped his watch and held it to his ear to check that it was still working. The sidelines were full but the energy was low. If a pin had dropped, it would have echoed between the parents standing like bowling pins on the sidelines. Their bodies were present, but their minds were absent.

Have you ever been to a youth soccer game where the weeds growing behind the goal made more noise than the parents on the touchlines? Or the arguments of the coaches and parents drowned out the cheering? Just what does parental cheering and participation in youth soccer mean, and does it really matter to the outcome of the game, or more important, to the ultimate development of your child?

What Does Cheering Do?

Medically speaking, excitement and encouragement heighten the release of adrenaline, which is stored in little bubblelike vesicles. When released into the brain and bloodstream, adrenaline increases alertness, muscle tone, readiness, pupillary size, breathing capacity, and cardiac output. All these physical reactions are needed for the human body to react optimally to the environment. In other words, when excitement and encouragement release adrenaline and other hormones into our system, we get stimulated to a state of peak psychological and physiological readiness, prepared for any eventuality.

In simpler terms, you can tell if children are at their best by the skip to their step, the gleam in their eye, and the sunshine in their smile. To doctors, that skip is the adrenaline in their arteries going to their muscles, that gleam is the epinephrine in their wide eyes, and that smile is the limbic emotional brain saying this is fun. *Cutting edge, momentum, intensity, focus,* and *concentration* are not just words, they are actual body reactions.

Ebb and Flow of the Game

It was the first half, and the Eagles' parents were huddled together along the touchline, full of anticipation, their eyes riveted on their own youngsters. The Eagles' striker scored, and the parents cheered. Then the Eagles' goalkeeper made an excellent save. The parents were on their feet waving, clapping, hooting with joy. Each Eagle's parent beamed with pride. The little soccer players with bright yellow shirts stood proud. They ran around the field, each with a spring in his step. The adrenaline was flowing, the epinephrine coursing through every muscle.

Later, in the dying minutes of the game, the Eagles were defending again, the score 4–4. The Lions had scored all four of their goals in the last ten minutes. The Lions' parents were in a frenzy. Sparks of their enthusiasm ignited their little players. Their striker ran into the Eagles' penalty area with determination. Adrenaline coursed through his arteries, fed by the Lions' parents and coaches chanting praise and encouragement: "Shoot! Shoot!"

On the opposite touchline, a gray cloud hung over the Eagles' parents. Their faces had turned sour. The Eagles themselves were slump-shouldered, already accepting defeat. The parents weren't conscious of it, but they were conveying a definite message to the Eagles. The juice, the momentum was gone—the smell of defeat saturated the air. Had the parents' behavior affected the children, or the children's playing affected the parents?

Three Cheers for Cheering

Labeling these kids as "losers" is an easy out. Sure, what these children needed was obvious, at least in hindsight, but how many times have you cheered your team on when it was losing? Logically—which is how adults think—one would not cheer if the Galaxy or Team USA or the home team were getting trounced and had lost its juice. Logically, then, one also would not cheer—meaning, be happy—when one's own kids were getting beaten. The problem is that children do not understand logic the way we grown-ups do. Losing is just not as important to them as it is to us. They are more interested in the fun of playing the game and having something to be happy about. When we tell them differently by our disapproving mood, who really loses—our kids or us? Who has their priorities right, who is being logical? We know that cheering and encouragement turn up adrenaline, which gives the children spirit and focus to do their best. Logically, then, when we do not cheer, we are the ones being illogical.

Cheering is not simply a way of rejoicing when the team is doing well; it is a way of showing acceptance and love and giving children a vote of confidence—*especially* when things are not going as hoped.

Children Need Praise the Most When They Appear to Deserve It the Least

What a child thinks of himself (his self-concept) depends on what his mom, dad, and other significant adults, such as coaches, reflect back to him. This is why some children are so confident in themselves despite their shortcomings, while others are so discouraged about their abilities despite all their gifts. Cheering when the child or team is doing well is also definitely important, of course, as it encourages repetition of the behavior and enhances self-confidence.

Cheering when your team is down is even more important, though, because it specifically augments the physiological response that increases physical prowess, to make your child the best he can be. In other words, cheering *is* the home advantage.

Cheering Is Winning

After my second year as a coach, I could plainly see that children with positive, participating parents had winning teams. Pick the right parents and you had a team that loved to play, a team where everyone looked forward to returning the next season.

To me, a winning team consisted of parents who would bring love, affection, and a touch of tenderness to their kids. The children were secure and cooperative with their friends. Nothing was boring to them. They seemed to have it all because their parents were always at their sides to guide and mold them into beautiful, harmonious sculptures with genuine grins and hearts full of contentment.

These children did not cringe with grief because they missed an easy shot or made a bad pass. They knew that if they made the effort they would always be rewarded. Their parents' cheers were not rewards for the goals scored or the plays made; they were hymns of support, trumpets of solidarity behind their children. The glee that emanated from these kids as the soccer season rolled on was the music that made me come back to coach.

From the Doctor's Desk

Cheering has certain senses:

1. The visual: a smile, a look that says, "Hey, you're my child and I'm proud!"
2. A sound: one that resonates warmth, encouragement, and has a beat full of heart and excitement.
3. A voice: words that are positive.
4. Cheering is the choir of harmony.
5. Cheering keeps children focused.
6. A cheering routine minimizes the problems that cause children anxiety and lead to inattention and confusion. (Jeering must not be permitted. It is the discord that has no place in youth soccer.)

19

The Cell Phone Invaders

The 19th Life Lesson:
There's One Team Ringer That's Really a Loser

The referee's whistle signaled a penalty in the final moments of a tied game. Every parent and coach was on the edge of his seat. I was biting the last of my nails—it had already been that tense a game. The goalkeeper swallowed nervously as beads of sweat glistened on his forehead. The whole game was hanging in the balance. The striker took a deep breath, clenched his little fists, and prepared to take his kick. Just then, a shrill, persistent ring shattered the atmosphere, breaking everyone's concentration.

You may remember the old sci-fi flick *Invasion of the Body Snatchers*. Now, with the popularity of wireless phones, we are in the era of the "invasion of the cell phones." Once it was only cheers and shouts of excitement that could be heard on a soccer field. Then cell phones invaded the game. Even those parents that do care enough to come to the field can now be found talking on their cellular phones rather than watching the game.

How are coaches and referees supposed to deal with this? Once we could throw someone out of a game, be it a player, coach, or unruly fan. But what do we do about throwing out these cell phones that are more invasive and troublesome than they are ever helpful to players on the field? They are not part of soccer and communicate only one thing to your children: They are less important than the phone. A study at the University of Southern California showed that a continually ringing cell phone increases the anxiety of parents and children. This will reduce a child's adrenaline and therefore his preparedness.

Stephen, the goalkeeper, finally got his father to come and watch him play soccer. But when he looked up midway through the game, his father was on his cell phone, talking hurriedly, one finger in his ear, his head turned away from the game. Stephen made an excellent save from a free kick, but his father's attention was elsewhere. His expression changed from jubilation at his great play to disappointment when he realized his father had missed it.

From the Doctor's Desk

The function of cell phones must be kept in perspective.

1. Unless there is a good reason, cell phones should be left in the car. Just having a cell phone handy prompts people to use them unnecessarily.
2. Cell phones are there for our convenience, not the other way around.
3. If you must carry a cell phone with you, put it on vibrate.

Nothing breaks up the atmosphere of a game quicker than a cacophony of ringing cell phones.

4. At the first parents meeting, coaches should insist that parents use their phones judiciously during games and should themselves of course refrain from using one.

20

Violence

The 20th Life Lesson:
Fighting Fire with Fire Only Leaves Ashes

I glanced anxiously at my watch. It was 10:25 and I was already twenty-five minutes late for the office and had not eaten breakfast yet. I turned my attention back to the road. God, couldn't this driver decide which lane she wanted? I stepped on the accelerator of my 150 horsepower VW Beetle, edging it forward in the heavy traffic. Suddenly, a Mercedes burst out of nowhere and shot in front of me, almost forcing me into the back of Mrs. Slowpoke. I slammed on the brakes. A gush of expletives exploded from my mouth. I gripped the steering wheel tightly, wishing it were the neck of that Mercedes' driver. Only ten minutes before as a rational physician I spoke to medical students on the art of patience.

My pulse slowly dropped back from two hundred to eighty and the cussing and ranting ceased. I returned from my state of temporary insanity, or "road rage" as it's called. We've all been there. If you haven't, then you've never driven in LA.

Unfortunately, I've seen this same rage on too many soccer

and Little League fields, the most inappropriate place for parents to lose their sanity. In Little League I call it "Little League Lunacy" or in soccer, "Soccer Savagery." If you've played or been involved in youth sports, you've almost certainly seen or done it yourself. A game, a carefree, enjoyable pastime, brings some people to the brink of homicide.

How does a children's sport like soccer bring out the worst? I'm not talking about violent criminals or convicted felons, but rather, normal, everyday people: Mom and Dad, Grandma and Grandpa, or experienced youth coaches. I know many of you are shaking your head right now, saying, "Not me, I'm not capable of behaving like that." But if you are a conscientious, loving, and devoted parent, you fit the profile of the "Soccer Savage."

Just Another Game

Bill, coach of the Peaches, wiped the sweat from his brow as he drove to Sidney Soccer Field for the evening girls-under-twelve game against the Blue Bonnets. But Bill, a plumber, had his mind elsewhere. He was still fuming about the last client he'd seen, who'd refused to pay his invoice. The client told Bill that he charged more than a doctor but had "half the brains of a gorilla."

At about the same time, Debra, coach of the Blue Bonnets, was also battling traffic, her thoughts firmly with her chauvinistic boss who had just threatened to fire her again. He was in one of those moods that came over him every time a deal fell through. And Debra, as usual, bore the brunt of his temper.

The game itself was as hot as the evening was humid, and Debra and Bill's moods did nothing to cool it down. Then it happened. A match was dropped into the kindling. Debra heard, or at least thought she heard, Bill threaten one of her players, specifically her daughter. She yelled at the referee about it, calling Bill a dimwitted ox. Barely had the words left her mouth, when Bill's face turned five shades of crimson, lightning exploded from between his teeth, and he raced across the field toward Debra. She grabbed hurriedly for her pepper spray. The result was irrational, irreverent, and devastating to the small children watching. The referee was bewildered, stunned into silence, as Debra unexpectedly blasted Bill with pepper spray.

An occurrence this extreme is, thankfully, not frequent, but once a season is too often. There are, however, many lesser conflicts that still inflict terrible damage on the youth soccer experience. Bill and Debra were not hostile people. They were nothing like Hank, a coach who had the ability to bring out the worst in people. Why then did it happen?

The Reasons for Soccer Savagery

There are four major factors that ignite such insanity in normally sane people.

1. Primordial protection. Parents have a biologically protective instinct over their children. This is especially strong in women.
2. A perceived injustice.
3. An attack on one's pride and prowess. This is especially strong in men.
4. Limbic neocortal overload. This is the short fuse that causes rational, responsible parents to go "nuts," that is, say and do insane things in the most inappropriate place, a child's soccer game.

Three Steps to Biological Explosion

Just as with an atomic bomb, there are defined steps before detonation. In me, the road rager, or you, the Little League lunatic or soccer savage, additive emotions provoke overreaction:

1. The stressful day (who doesn't have one?) increases one's adrenaline and therefore aggressiveness. Stress also decreases serotonin, a neurotransmitter that governs social control of the neocortex or thinking brain.

2. Fatigue or hunger (games are often played before dinner) activates the hypothalamus (central part of the brain next to the rage area) for "fight or flight." This is why it's never a good idea to step into the cage when the lion is hungry—or to drive in front of me before I've had breakfast.

3. For the involuntary part of the brain in charge of rage to take over, one often needs to depersonalize the perceived foe through name calling and other depersonalizing activities. This allows a loss of social respect and frontal lobe control of our brain.

4. Perceived injustice or threat is the final straw that ignites the explosion of the limbic unconscious brain, causing a complete loss of neocortex control and an outbreak of violence.

Debra and Bill Revisited

Primordial protection was the major factor effecting Debra. In contrast with Bill it was pride. Both had experienced a stressful day and both were hungry, which increased their adrenaline by the time they reached the field. Debra's primordial protective instinct for her daughter caused her to react appropriately by telling the referee. But then, she took an extra unnecessary step that was borne of her instinct to protect her child. She depersonalized Bill by demeaning him and calling him a dimwitted ox. Bill's pride and prowess was offended. This was a weak spot for Bill because he never did well in school. He perceived an injustice because someone belittled him in front of others. He lost his cool (neocortical control) and his animal instincts (limbic brain) propelled him across the field.

For most of the children, it was the first time they'd seen violent conflict between adults. The most damaging aspect of the incident was the bad and very sad example it set for the children.

An Ounce of Prevention Is Better Than a Pound of Cure

How can parents and coaches deal with this?

1. Set up a friendly environment. Give opposing sides a chance to meet. Parents from each side should mix and shake hands with each other. Meeting, speaking, and mingling with the other side prevents depersonalization and reduces the possibility of perceiving them as a threat.

2. Before assuming an injustice, ask the referee for clarification. Debra thought she heard Bill call her daughter a "pushy bitch." The referee heard him say "push up, Peaches."

3. Know your warning signs. Have something to eat before the game. If your hands are clenched or your teeth gritted, it's a sure sign you're in the "pre-detonation" phase. Walk away

from the field, take a deep breath, and count to ten.

4. Remember, never confront someone after the game (when most fights begin) if you or they are "hot" after a perceived injustice. Talk to the referee, call him on the phone later if you have to, or talk to the regional commissioner. Better still, just let it go.

5. Always remember that it's a game and remind everyone else that they are there to have fun with their child and to be an example of honesty and goodwill to the children.

6. As a fail-safe plan, have a mantra: "The family that kicks together, sticks together."

What About Courage?

I know many of you must be saying, but Dr. Fortanasce, you told us to have courage against the intolerable! What are you saying now?

I'm saying that you should know the difference between courage and confrontation. Courage also requires tact, which is knowing the appropriate time and place. Confrontation is approaching a problem from an offensive or incendiary attacking position. Confrontation is like fighting fire with fire: It only leads to ashes.

 From the Doctor's Desk

There are thirteen key points to remember.

The four basic factors that can bring out the worst in adult behavior are:

1. Primordial protection. Parents are biologically protective of their children. This is especially strong in women.
2. Perceived injustice.
3. Pride and prowess. Especially strong in men.
4. Biological reaction (neocortal limbic violence system or "fight-or-flight" reaction).

Additive emotions provoke overreaction:

5. Stressful day: increase in adrenaline and aggressiveness, decrease in serotonin due to stress provokes loss of social control.
6. Fatigue and hunger activates the hypothalamus rage area for "fight or flight."
7. Depersonalization (name calling) allows loss of social respect.
8. Perceived threat provokes limbic explosion causing complete loss of neocortex control and outbreak of violence.

Head off the threat of violence by:

9. Shaking hands with the other parents. Meeting, speaking, and mingling with the other side means neither they nor you will be depersonalized and perceived as a threat.
10. Before assuming an injustice has been done, ask the referee for clarification.
11. Know your warning signs. Take a breath, count to ten, walk away, and say, "The family that kicks together, sticks together." Or "Soccer is a sweet song."
12. Never confront someone after the game if you or he is hot after a perceived injustice. Talk to the referee, the coach, or the regional commissioner.

13. Always remember that it's a game and remind everyone else why he is there: to be an example of honesty and goodwill to the children.

PART V

PARENTING

I never knew what life was all about, what the world meant, until I had a child and held him in my arms. I never realized how wonderful a smile could be until my child smiled at me. When I kicked the ball and my child returned it a new bond was born. The world was more wonderful and fulfilling than I ever thought. Now I understand what the word *parent* truly means.

Remember, P-A-R-E-N-T stands for:

P: Presence. Be there for your child, show you care.
A: Attitude. Be positive. Use five compliments for every one criticism.
R: Respect, for referees, coaches, and other children.
E: Example. Be on your best behavior in front of your child.
N: Nurturing. Accept and encourage your child's efforts.
T: Tolerant. Don't take mistakes seriously. This is just one step in your child's life, so make it one he'll remember fondly.

21

Parent Power

The 21st Life Lesson:
Know the Myths of Parenting

A good sauce takes time,
A great kid takes patience
—MOMMA FORTANASCE

The phone startled me out of a deep sleep. Rubbing my eyes, I stretched over to pick it up.

"Hi, Uncle Vin? It's me, Mark. I didn't want to wake you too early. It's 8:15 in the morning there, isn't it? We just had a son! I can't begin to describe the feeling. When I held him in my arms and gazed into his eyes, for the first time, I realized what life is all about."

I checked the clock next to my bed. It was 2:15 A.M., California time. My nephew used to have great ball sense as a child, but never any sense of time. "I've already gotten him a soccer ball," he went on. "I just can't wait to get him out of the nursery and onto the soccer field." That line snapped me wide awake. The ecstasy in Mark's voice, the joy, the hope—I knew Mark was experiencing the very same emotions I had when my first son, Vinny, was born. As soon as I realized he was born, I began fantasizing about kicking a soccer ball or tossing a baseball to him—the beginning of bonding, the formation of an inseparable link between parent and child.

The soccer or baseball field becomes their first common ground. It is a time for sharing and building memories, for parents to impart their knowledge to their children. Soccer and baseball are about more than a ball being knocked to and fro—they are about love and acceptance being passed back and forth. My father once told me, "You never know the meaning of life, of love, until you have a child to play ball with."

Yes, I knew what my nephew was feeling and dreaming. I also knew that once his new baby son came home, Mark's life would change in ways he probably had not imagined: sleepless nights, wet diapers, endless feedings. For the time being, though, Mark was on cloud nine and I wasn't going to disturb him. As I congratulated him and hung up, I put my arms behind my head, slowly closed my eyes, and remembered how I had looked forward to being out there with my son that first time.

Not the Best, Not the Worst—Just the Reality

My first memory of Vinny was not on the soccer field, but like many fathers of my generation, on the baseball diamond. It seems like only yesterday that he held my thumb as I led him onto the diamond of dreams. His baseball cap was skewed sideways and his glove dragged by his side, but he had a skip to his step and a sparkle in his eye. And I cannot even describe the jumble of feelings I had.

Little League tryouts were in two weeks. I would train my son just the way my dad had trained me. Vinny stood there, grinning, and pounded his tiny fist into the glove as he had seen me do so many times. I threw the first ball and watched it bounce toward him. His eyes glued to the ball, he snagged it at just the right moment, then threw a perfect strike.

Oh, God, I thought, if this is not heaven, what is? In the recesses of my brain, I heard the major-league loudspeaker at Dodger Stadium: "And in the stands today is Dr. Vince Fortanasce, here to see his all-star son playing third base and cleanup batter." I heard the chatter and cheers of the fans. I looked back at my son and pictured him in Dodger blue. I swear I could see a little ember of light in his big brown eyes.

My next toss was a little harder. Vinny scooped it up again but this time threw it ten feet wide. I retrieved the ball and approached him with a look of concern. I explained how to throw the ball straight and what the consequences of a bad throw were. "A bad throw is an error," I told him. "And that's bad."

I increased the speed of my next throw, giving Vinny a one-bouncer. The ball careened off the heel of his glove then off his chest. Without a whimper, he picked it up and threw it back—again, about ten feet wide. I walked over and instructed him on the art of catching a one-bouncer, and the importance of preventing a ball from getting by. "If you do, it's an error," I remember saying.

Another toss, Vinny picked it off as I'd told him to, but instead of throwing the ball, he just held it. "Vinny, throw the ball," I yelled. He just looked at me and shook his head. I shouted at him again to throw the ball. He just looked at me and I noticed then that the sparkle had disappeared from his eyes.

"Dad," he said, "let's go. I don't want to make errors." Fatherly (and a little annoyed), I stomped over and told him he'd never be a good ballplayer if he didn't practice. "But Daddy, I want to go home."

I refused and told him we were going to play for at least another thirty minutes, until he got it right. "Tryouts are only two weeks away," I impressed upon him. It was time for Vinny to learn some discipline. Then I realized that my own grin had turned into a grimace.

I reached back and flung the next ball to him. He simply stood there and let the ball fly straight past his shoulder. "Vinny!" I shouted loud enough to be heard across the ball field. "What is wrong with you?" In answer, he started to giggle and dance about like a marionette being pulled by strings. "Stop acting stupid," I snapped. But this only spurred him on to more puppet play. As I briskly walked past him to fetch the ball, I saw my dreams melting into pools of disappointment. The ember of sunshine in his eyes had been extinguished.

When I arrived home after work the next day, I found Vinny and suggested we go out to play. He said he couldn't find his glove. I told him where it was and waited by the door for him to fetch it. When I didn't hear him coming, I went to look for him. He was standing in front of the TV, watching the same show I had just told him to turn off. Disappointment—no, hurt—overwhelmed me. My son did not care for me. He did not want to play with his own father. He didn't care about getting ready for tryouts. He had no discipline! How could this have happened?

Need I really explain?

Vinny's puppet routine was a strong, nonverbal message: "Dad, please like me. Please smile. Look, look, I'm a puppet, here to entertain you." He had been trying his best, but his best was not good enough for me. My dream of playing ball with my son back in his Little League and soccer days was not marred due to lack of discipline, but because my tone and expressions clearly told him I was withdrawing my acceptance and love. He had no idea what "preparing for tryouts" meant—all he wanted was to have a good time with his dad. He did not want to hurt me by making an "error."

Each of my children had a different nonverbal way of giving me the same message. My daughter, Kaycee, would become stubborn and deliberately make the same mistake over and over whenever she felt she was not getting a favorable response from me. Michael, though, was the most difficult of all. He developed a pattern of behavior that told me, loud and clear, "Hey, Dad, lighten up!" He began to twitch his neck and grimace, occasionally letting out a little *cheep,* like a bird. Being a neurologist, I suspected this was Tourette's syndrome, a neurological disorder characterized by sudden, uncontrollable mannerisms, such as twitching or tics associated with unusual vocalizations. I quickly brought Michael in to see my partner, Charlie, a pediatric neurologist. Luckily, it was not Tourette's syndrome at all, just a nervous habit that went away when I changed my behavior!

My interactions with Vinny, Kaycee, and Michael turned out to be mild compared with some of the things I saw. Tellingly, it was not the disinterested mothers and fathers, but the dedicated ones who tried hardest with their children and had been soccer or baseball aficionados all their lives, who seemed to have the hardest time. Those with the greatest expectations had the greatest problems.

A Bitter Fact to Face

Tri, one of my closest friends, and I coached our first soccer team together. His son, Patrick, was such an obedient child—until Tri tried to teach him to play, that is. Suddenly, dutiful little Patrick would turn into a stone-faced zombie staring straight ahead as Tri attempted to talk to him, and wound up talking to himself. "Why won't he listen? Why won't he try?" Why, indeed!

After two practices, Vinny played center alongside Patrick. At the start of practice, Vinny and Patrick looked and acted just like our sons, but as the session progressed, a distressing metamorphosis occurred. Vinny turned from an attentive ballplayer into a giggling puppet, while Patrick, a skillful tackler, degenerated into a mummified corpse. When we asked them what was wrong, they said, "Nothing." Did they want to play? "Oh, sure," they both said, with all the enthusiasm of a child waiting for the dentist's drill.

My wife, Arlene, and Tri's wife soon became concerned about how their sons forced themselves to the soccer field. I clearly remember the day it all came to a head. Vinny and I had just gotten home from practice when my wife cornered me. "Vinny told me he doesn't like soccer," she said. "He doesn't want to play. I think you are the reason he doesn't like it. If you can't change how you treat him, I'm going to pull him out."

"Pull him out? Pull him out! *Pull him out!*" The words reverberated in my head. This was far beyond a personal crisis—it was more like the end of the world! I could not imagine living without a boy in soccer. Yes, I know it sounds stupid. Imagine me, a doctor, who deals with life-and-death situations every day, not knowing that life is more than sports. But deep down, I cherished that stupid dream of being announced over the stadium loudspeaker as the father of superstar player Vinny Fortanasce—playing in Wembley Stadium for the World Cup Final. Arlene's ultimatum made me feel as if I were facing Armageddon, but it also forced me to make a decision.

Deep down, I knew she was right, because I could see so clearly what Tri was doing wrong. Good Lord, you would've thought he was training professional soccer players out there. He never applauded Patrick's successes, only reinforced his mistakes. Yet, with my son and the other boys, Tri was a model of patience, positive attitude, and support. I, too, had nothing but praise and patience for the rest of the team, but was doing exactly the same thing with Vinny that Tri was doing with Patrick. Looking back now, I realize I had been living a myth or, rather, several myths.

The Myths of Parenting

If parents can counteract the four myths of parenting, their experience (not expectations) with youth soccer can be something they and their child will always cherish.

The four myths are:

1. Every child will naturally love soccer, baseball, or whatever sport I love.
2. A child will love playing soccer with his parents.
3. Children will always tell the truth.

4. A parent is the best teacher for his or her child.

Myth One: Every child will naturally love soccer, baseball, or whatever sport I love.

This lies only in the mind of the parent. As children become older, especially by the time they are teenagers, it is clear that they have minds of their own. However, when they are five to nine you exert a great deal of influence. From ten to twelve your influence is substantial but is beginning to wane. That influence can be used to either push a child away or pull him closer to "what you want" for him.

Children will love soccer or any sport their parents love if they get their mom and dad's approval and attention. Teens, however, seek approval primarily from their peers and so will love whatever their peers love. If that is doing drugs or joining a gang, they will be drawn in that direction. If it is playing soccer, baseball, or another team sport, they will gravitate toward these more wholesome endeavors. Five- to twelve-year-olds love to imitate and follow their parents. So if you hang around the soccer field and engage them in sports, chances are they will follow you and continue that legacy with their children. But if you drop them off as you would at a baby-sitter, they will see that you value neither soccer nor them.

My frowns, my dissatisfaction and stern lectures, however well meaning, did not give Vinny the idea that I approved of or liked him. Children establish their own self-worth through our reactions to them. Remember, we smile and they smile. When we frown they think they are bad and we will cause them to dislike the things we like.

Myth Two: A child will love playing soccer with his parents.

Mary's face peered from the touchline, tear-stained, riddled with anguish. Her daughter, Sylvia, was trudging unenthusiastically around the midfield, a similar expression on her face. After the game, I donned my psychiatrist's persona and asked Mary if everything was OK. "Oh, yes," she stuttered with a mix of doom and anxiety. Amazing, I thought, how we always try to present an unruffled facade despite the obvious turmoil raging underneath. I knew Mary well, so I felt comfortable pressing the issue. I asked her again, adding, "I noticed Sylvia's upset, too." With that, Mary broke down and told me she felt her daughter didn't care for her.

The First Greeting

Mary is a working mom and felt that Sylvia held more affection for the baby-sitter than for her. I recounted a few observations I'd made of their relationship. Mary rarely smiled at her daughter. I'd heard her talk to Sylvia about cleaning her room, finishing her homework, and a host of other justifiable concerns, but nothing else. I reminded her that a child's first greeting with the parent sets the tone for the rest of the day. If, when you first walk through the door in the evening, you smile, hug her, tell her how much you missed her, how much you're looking forward to playing with her, Sylvia will naturally love to be with you. The adage you'll catch more bees with honey than with vinegar, is especially true with children.

Homework and other chores are obviously important and can be tackled after you've connected and bonded with your child. In fact, after a good day together, my son will often ask if

I want to help him with his homework, and even once asked, "Can I throw out the garbage?"

Kids enjoy being and playing with their parents as long as they are having fun and it is pleasing their parents. They must be given encouragement, guidance, and respect for their efforts.

Myth Three: Children will always tell the truth.

For the most part, they do—unless they feel they will be punished or lose the parent's love.

Children naturally tell us what they think we want to hear in order to avoid trouble. In that, they are no different than the rest of us. Parents and coaches must be able to read the nonverbal messages that tell the real story. When Vinny couldn't find his soccer ball, then became easily distracted by the TV, he was sending me a message. I just wasn't "listening" to what he was showing me. The child develops this passive-aggressive technique when the parent makes an experience, in this case baseball, a negative one.

Each child has his or her own nonverbal means of communicating anxiety or anger. One child I knew would stick her tongue in her cheek when she was angry. When I asked her if she was chewing gum or eating, she would shake her head. Years later, when she was in high school, I learned she did this tongue-in-cheek routine whenever she got angry. It had started when she first stuck her tongue out at her dad and promptly received a spanking. To protect herself, she had developed this disguise technique that satisfied her need to express her anger and, at the same time, allowed her to avoid punishment. Some of the more frequent mannerisms children bring to our neurology clinic are tics, head twitching, and tongue clucking. Often these are just their nonverbal ways of communicating their tension.

Myth Four: A parent is the best teacher for his or her child.

This is true only if a parent has realistic expectations. Unrealistic expectations stem from a parent's having dreams for his or her child that the child can never realize or fulfill. Children do not start out sharing their parents' dreams and will never grow to share them unless they are treated with respect and love, regardless of whether they make mistakes.

Often their only expectation from soccer is to have fun. They will react positively if they receive their parents' and coaches' approval. One good rule of thumb when practicing with or teaching your child is to deal with their mistakes and faults as gently as you deal with your own; another is to do something to make your child smile when you are upset with him, *then* go back to the task at hand.

Give a Little, Get a Lot

If children don't want to do something we know is best for them, should we allow them this freedom?

If your dreams of playing soccer with your child are rapidly turning into a Stephen King nightmare, step back and take a little reality check. First, recognize the difference between what you think is the problem, and what the problem really is. I thought my problem with Vinny was his attitude, but it was actually my "anticipatory anxiety." I knew the tryouts were coming up, Vinny did not—even if he had, he would have had no concept of what they meant to me. I had gone through twenty-seven years of school always preparing for the next test. My anxious mind said, "What if Vinny isn't ready for the big test? He will be a failure the rest of his life. He will never learn discipline. He will never amount to anything. He will be a total flop!"

Yes, these were my problems. Vinny's problem was my frown and my tone of voice, which told him I did not approve of him. Vinny did not want to disappoint me, he wanted to stop playing so he would not hurt me anymore, and maybe do something else so that we could be friends again.

Time and Fun

Next, recognize your child's expectations to have fun and make you laugh. Children really do want to make their parents happy, so go ahead, have fun, roll in the grass, play games. Before you can encourage your child to do anything, play soccer or otherwise, he must learn to like you. If you are having fun, you will be fun to be with; if you are always serious and disapproving, you will be the last person he wants to be around. When you have fun together, your child will soon want to be like you, because you love and accept him and want to be with him. Remember, just because a child is genetically yours, does not mean he will love or want to be with you.

Child rearing is like flying a kite, you must run gently at first, until the kite begins to soar on its own. Slowly you unwind the string, so it can fly higher. Once up, you reel the kite closer for a while or let out more string, depending on the wind. Like a kite, a child elevates to great heights when he or she goes against the current. The key is to let him fly on his own.

From the Doctor's Desk

1. Know your conscious and unconscious expectations. If you're unsure of what signals you are giving off, ask your spouse or a close friend, someone who'll tell you the truth, not just what you want to hear.

2. Make your child feel special when you first greet her each day, both verbally and nonverbally. A smile, a hug, an "I missed you."

3. Participate with your child; don't be just an observer.

4. Have fun and your child will be happy, win or lose.

5. Make shared memories by consistently being there and having a routine, like pizza after the game.

22

Parental Consistency

The 22nd Life Lesson:
Children Need Boundaries and
Parents Must Have Them to Give Them

Little Maryann was a handful. Her mother, Margaret, seemed to let her have free reign. If she wanted candy, she got it. If she wanted to quit in the middle of practice, she could. Charlie, her soccer coach, once asked Margaret why she let nine-year-old Maryann do whatever she wanted. She replied, "Children do best when left to their own will. It helps them build their own personality."

The following week, Margaret arrived at a soccer field where the Thunders would temporarily be practicing. She stared aghast at the overgrown field, at the weeds sprouting all over, and she turned to Charlie. "This field's a mess, it's running wild. Why don't they do something about it?"

Charlie smiled and said, "They're leaving the field to its own will. It's building its own personality."

Responsibility

Enrolling a child in soccer takes a commitment on your part.

Many parents forget who is the parent and who is the child. The ability of a coach to create harmony is dependent upon the parent showing control and setting boundaries for her children away from the soccer field. Children want and need boundaries in order to develop discipline and to become "something more." Yes, children really want a parent to be in control despite their words and actions that seem to say, "Leave me alone!"

Chucky

Chucky, a little on the chubby side, always seemed nervous and uncertain on the field. As the ball was played forward, Chucky began to run on to it, with only the opposition goalkeeper in front of him. Then he stopped, looking toward the linesman. The linesman had his flag down. "You're onside, Chucky," his coach shouted. "Run, run." Chucky chewed his lip anxiously. He couldn't decide what to do. Two defenders caught up with him and cleared the ball to safety. Chucky had missed an easy shot.

Anyone who knew Chucky's parents could understand why he was so uncertain, so indecisive. When his mother said yes, his father said no. Both his parents were either late to practice and the game or late to pick him up. On one occasion, his mother dropped him off with his father and told him he was not to eat ice cream after the game.

Later, I went to the local ice cream shop where I saw Chucky and his dad. Chucky said to his father, "Mom said I shouldn't have any ice cream. I have to watch my weight."

His dad replied, "What does Mom know? This won't hurt you. It'll build muscle."

Consistency

When we think of consistency, we often think of the player who scores every game, the goalkeeper who shuts out the opposition regularly, or the player or coach who is on time for every practice. However, a parent's consistency is also key. It is as essential for the development of a child's self-confidence, conscience, and character as food and water is to his physical growth. Regardless of whether parents are strict or liberal (as long as it's not extreme in either case), they should be that way consistently, and both parents should agree on the boundaries and rules for their children. Parents must support one another.

By knowing and witnessing what a parent feels is right and wrong, and what a parent will or will not tolerate, a child understands, unquestionably, what is expected of her and derives a sense of comfort from knowing what to expect. It is better that they learn this from a sympathetic parent at an early age rather than, for example, a less sympathetic boss later on.

Single Parents

Twenty-five percent of all families in America are single-parent families. Most are headed by the mother. Seventy-three percent of those mothers must work. Despite the tremendous pressure on these women, several studies have shown the single mothers to be well adjusted. A major problem preventing that adjustment, however, is their ability to be consistent and communicate their needs to their children.

Sacha

Sacha was proudly showing her little soccer teammates the expensive new soccer cleats and gold bracelet her mother had just bought her. Her mother, Dotty, was a single parent who held down a part-time job at the local Hallmark store. She had little money to spend on luxury items like these. But, despite their financial constraints, Sacha showed little concern for being thrifty and rarely smiled in appreciation of the gifts her mother gave her. Her reaction to the new boots and bracelet was so unusual that her dutiful mother felt justified at the sacrifices she'd had to make to buy them.

I'm sure Dotty had good intentions but she was, in fact, confusing her daughter. They lived under financial constraints. Sacha's learning about their actual financial situation would not only imbue her with realistic expectations, but it would also make Dotty's life easier. When Sacha accepted that they did not have a lot of extra money and that Dotty's limitations reflected a lack of money, not a lack of love, she would not put Dotty in an awkward position of having to deny her things by asking for them. As a physician, I've seen many parents whose overindulgence of their children harms rather than helps them. This is particularly true of single parents who somehow feel their child has been shortchanged and must be compensated for it, or single parents who feel the need to compete with the other parent for the child's affection.

Children quickly pick up on such inconsistency and learn

to use one parent against the other. I often hear such kids using variations of the phrase, "If you won't get it for me, Daddy will. Daddy loves me more." The best response I heard was from a mother who said, "Well, I love you too. But I want to do what is right for you so you grow up to be healthy and independent. I'm sure your dad will agree. Let's ask him." Children with consistent parents have more fun in soccer, follow directions, and relate better with their teammates because they feel secure.

From the Doctor's Desk

Lack of consistency gets in the way of building the essential elements of making a child successful. Children know themselves by the boundaries we, the parents, make for them. They must know what is OK and what is not, and that must not vary according to our moods. There should be one unanimous message from parents and coaches to the child, one message that can be easily understood and interpreted by the child.

1. Children need boundaries to feel safe and cared for. It's your part in creating a harmonious environment for them.
2. Don't be persuaded by arguments such as: "Every other mom lets their kid do it," or, "But Dad said it was OK."
3. Parents, especially separated parents, must communicate when, how, and where the limits should be set.
4. If uncertain, answer: "Let's wait till I talk to your mom/dad/friends' parents."
5. If in doubt, always do what will make them a more honest, honorable, and healthy person.

6. Remember, saying no for a good reason teaches your child limits and the spirit behind the rules you've set. Saying, "Let's think about it more" lets them know you are listening. Yes may be the easy answer, but no might be the best one for them.

23

Virtual Insanity: Sports' Greatest Enemy

The 23rd Life Lesson:
The Family That Kicks Together, Sticks Together

Monica, our team captain and last season's top scorer, didn't show up for the first practice of the new soccer season. But her mother did. "She doesn't want to play," her mother reluctantly admitted. "I guess we can't force her. Kids must grow their own personalities." Gee, I thought, where have I heard that before?

Monica, it seems, had not discovered boys but had discovered the allure of "virtual reality." Playing video games, surfing the Net, and watching TV in her bedroom had taken over her life, and was now keeping her from soccer practice. Her mother was concerned but simply shrugged and said, "What can I do? She has a mind of her own."

I was puzzled. Why would Monica prefer the four walls of her room to the great outdoors, the cheering of the crowd, the camaraderie of her teammates? Then I remembered the final game of last season.

Monica missed an easy chance in the final minutes and we lost the game and the championship. I was disappointed. Very disappointed. I know I've said that winning is about effort, not about results, but I do like to win as well as teach kids the principles of character. Maybe I'd shown my disappointment a little too overtly. But if I was competitive, Monica's dad was impossible. His face would get so red with tension and anguish that I often thought it was close to erupting. He would shatter the harmony of any game with his constant and fervent screams of, "Go, Monica!" When she missed that late shot on goal and the championship was gone, I was certain I could see steam billowing from his ears.

Maybe the four walls of her room sheltered Monica from both me and her father.

A Problem of Tremendous Proportions

The reality is, parents need sitters, distractions for their kids, so that they can have some time to themselves. TV, the Internet, and video games provide ideal baby-sitters or ways to keep kids occupied while their parents take a break. In moderation, of course, these "virtual realities" can be harmless, even beneficial to children. However, the growing dependency parents have on TV, video, and the Net for occupying their children's time, represents a tremendous danger.

A recent survey by *Time* magazine listed the amount of time the average child spends watching TV, playing video games, and surfing the Net compared to the amount of time he spends doing homework, playing sports, and engaging in family activities. The results were shocking. Fifty percent of children spend more than four hours a day occupied in these "virtual realities," while more than 20 percent admit that their parents would strongly disagree with what they're watching or playing.

A sport like soccer is not just a healthy way to teach children character and values but, just as important, it is a way to teach socialization skills and develop a child's emotional intelligence. The greatest enemy to organized youth sports like soccer is not gangs or the dissolution of the family through divorce, but video games, television, and the Internet.

The "In Thing"

Tony's mom knocked on the door again. "Tony, how many times have I told you not to lock your door!" she called out. Tony, just nine years old, inched the door open, his face flushed with embarrassment. His mom had almost caught him surfing porn pages on the Internet. No, Tony didn't quite understand what it was all about, only that the older kids at school seemed to think it was cool, the "in thing" to do. Even at Tony's age, it's important to be "in." After all, shouldn't the older kids know what's best?

Children do know when they are doing something wrong and it just takes common sense to spot it. If your child usually keeps his bedroom door open, why is it now closed? If it's usually closed but unlocked, why is it now locked? Don't be accusatory but let your child know that it is OK to be inquisitive about sex and maybe show him some more appropriate sex education material. It's also a good idea to notify their friends' parents.

OK, Now You've Gone Too Far

So you think this is too much? Well ask yourself this: If someone called you to say that your nine-year-old may be surfing porn sites on the Internet, would you be upset?

Tony's mom called Tony's best friend's mother and told her what Tony was doing, and since he and Sam were best friends, Sam might be doing the same. She asked Sam's mom to handle it discreetly, she didn't want Tony embarrassed, but at the same time she didn't want Sam and Tony encouraging each other in this activity. She suggested they install filtering software which helps keep out inappropriate material, but is not a guarantee that it won't find its way into the home, on the boys' computers. Then she added, "Maybe this weekend we can take the boys to see the Women's World Cup soccer team play, as a way of refocusing their attention on soccer.

Remember, on subjects like this, children don't need to be condemned or frightened but rather need to know what you think is right and wrong, and what you think is healthy for them to be seeing on the Net. Soon enough they'll be teenagers and your influence on what they view will diminish greatly.

The Pros and Cons of TV, Video Games, and the Net

The Internet and other "virtual" activities spark a child's imagination and help to develop important hand-eye coordination. The Net is a fantastic research and learning tool, an at-home library with a wealth of stimulating information on every conceivable subject. Video games, too, can be informative and provide important learning skills.

Video games and the Net are a great way for extroverted children to learn to be by themselves and work independently. For introverted kids, the danger is that they can become increasingly isolated by participating in these activities.

For introverts, extroverts, and every child in between, too much of any "virtual reality" can be disastrous.

1. A child who spends too much time alone in his room will experience a decrease in socialization skills.
2. TV and video games are often devoid of character principles and values.
3. Many video games and TV shows glorify violence and senseless combat and promote a disrespect for and defiance of authority.
4. Many video games are repetitive and without functional value.
5. Certain information available on the Net may be totally unsuitable for children.

How Much Is Too Much?

"Todd had to be called five times to come down to dinner." Skip's anguish was building. He was concerned about his eleven-year-old son. "Every day it's the same," he went on. "He comes home, drops his books on the floor, then disappears into his bedroom to play the latest video game."

"He looks pale, his eyes are dull, he gets tired quickly, and worst of all he's like a rubber band, ready to snap." From a neurological standpoint, what Skip was seeing in his son was "shell shock," similar to what soldiers experience after being constantly bombarded with stress, adrenaline continually pumping to keep them alert, ready for any impending threat.

Playing video games for sustained periods has a similar effect on a child's body, exhausting the adrenaline and serotonin stores, leaving the child behaving like he hasn't slept for days. Attention and enthusiasm decrease after being constantly prepared for the next wave of video "bad guys" or monsters to attack. In most video games, the more successful the player is, the better the enemy becomes, which only adds to the levels of stress.

I know Hank might jump in here and say, "It makes kids ready for life, because life always gets harder as you grow up. It keeps them vigilant." Well, Hank, that's OK for soldiers, but not for children. A small dose of this may not be bad, but the effects of prolonged exposure are all negative. Some video games increase a child's motor development and teach useful survival techniques. But many, and often the most popular, are destructive both in content and how they affect children. Parents and coaches must always be on the lookout for the physical signs that a child is overindulging in these activities: increased shyness, dull eyes, easily fatigued, increased anxiety.

Remember, statistics show that those children who play active sports are 57 percent more likely to finish high school; 40 percent more likely to go to college; 37 percent less likely to become involved in delinquent behavior at school; and 88 percent less likely to be negatively involved with the police.

From the Doctor's Desk

1. Time for watching TV, surfing the Net, and playing video games (especially violent video games) should be closely monitored and a child should be told how much time is allowed for such activity. Perhaps you could write it down on a family plan board, a chalkboard that hangs in the kitchen or other common room.

2. Children should not have TVs in their own rooms. It seriously interferes with family socialization and a parent's ability to influence a child's values. Establish a time for them to watch TV after their homework is completed and you have reviewed it.

3. Watching TV and videos should be a time for the family to gather together, enjoy sports, movies, sitcoms, and educational programs as a family. Parents should learn to enjoy children's TV shows, especially when your kids are in their teens. It will increase your ability to communicate with your child.

Parents who allow their children to have a TV, video games, and access to the Net in their rooms, have a grave responsibility to also ensure their children spend more time in socialization with the family and other children. If not, then prepare to pay the consequences. Children can be hooked onto things other than drugs. It may not be lethal, but it is potentially dangerous to their development and could destroy their potential for future success.

Family dinners are a great way to wind down from a day, and provide an especially good opportunity for discussing soccer; playing hard can be brought up and encouraged, and winning can be de-emphasized.

24

Joining In

The 24th Life Lesson:
You Must Be a Friend to Make a Friend

Derrick was a loner, a quiet but gentle child of eight. His mother told me how she frequently tried to get him to join in games with other kids, but that he just seemed not to know how. He was only content in front of the TV or playing video games. "Seems strange," she said, "he doesn't know how to make friends." Then she recounted the following story.

While Derrick was in the park with his mother, he saw two other boys kicking a soccer ball to each other. His mom encouraged him to join in. He ran over to the two boys playing and grabbed the ball and just stood there, unsure what to do next. One of the other kids angrily shouted, "No!" and snatched the ball back from him. Derrick walked back over to his mom with tears in his eyes and told her he wanted to go home.

Sense of Belonging

Most parents assume a child knows how to make friends and join in with other children. Some, like Derrick, don't know how. When he got home, Derrick returned to the comfort of his room and the TV. All children need a sense of belonging, a sense that they are part of "something." If a child's parents are too busy, if he cannot make friends on his own, that "something" becomes surrogate friends in the shape of TV and video games, "friends" that he will always be able to get along with, and ones that will never reject or yell at him.

Fitting In

Is it natural for people to know how to make friends? I'm sure most people can think of someone at work who is just not a "people person." Today's youth (due in part to modern technology like the Internet that encourages solitary participation and negates the need for human contact) are not learning how to interact socially. Imagine how most adults make first contact:

"Hi, Vince Fortanasce," I say with a smile as I extend my hand.

"Walt O'Grady," the man replies.

"O'Grady," I repeat. "An Irish name."

"Yes," he beams. "Family's originally from Dublin. And you—is that a New York accent?"

"Yeah, I grew up on Long Island."

"Oh, me too."

Adults have a whole ritual of contact. The handshake, which tells so much about a person, the name, place of birth, homing in on similarities and looking for common ground are all techniques adults use to fit in and make friends.

Social Graces

Imagine meeting someone new, staring him in the face, and saying, "What do you want? Who do you think you are? Are you good enough to be around me? Are you a threat?" Derrick, in fact, did just that by running up to the two boys playing soccer and grabbing their ball. There was no nonverbal first contact like a smile or a handshake and no common ground established. Consequently, his friendly intentions were seen as threatening.

Such social graces are not inherited. Derrick was a sensitive boy with a high emotional potential, but had never been taught how to behave in a social situation. He had no siblings and at school spent lunch break alone.

Sammy, on the other hand, was introduced to youth sports through his older brothers. I watched him meander up to the touchline as a group of boys played soccer. You could almost hear the wheels turning in his head—how do I join in? When the ball went out of bounds near him, he picked it up and threw it to one of the older boys on the field. "Hi, my name's Sammy. I play soccer, too. D'you need another player? I see you haven't got a goalkeeper. I could play there if you like."

Sammy was first helpful and showed good intentions, then declared a mutual interest in soccer. By observing the boys play, he noticed a position he could plug into. How could anyone resist such social graces?

Later in life, Sammy, in need of a job, might be required to demonstrate similar good intentions to the staff he meets at an interview, then make pertinent observations about the company and correctly identify a role he can plug into.

At this age it may only be soccer, but it can be the gateway to your child's future. Soccer offers access strategies for child-hood friendships and so much more.

Social Soccer

When Derrick's mother read of how children who play sports are 80 percent less likely to join gangs and twice as likely to go to college, she signed him up for American Youth Soccer Organization (AYSO). At the first practice, Derrick lurked on the sidelines, watching the other kids kick the ball around, but too scared to join in himself. Eventually, noting Derrick's reluc-tance, I walked over with a smile and handed him the ball on the touchline. "Here, you throw it in," I told him. Derrick did and then one of the others passed it back to him and Derrick kicked it back.

Derrick learned the key access strategy, the key lesson on how to participate. You must give in order to get; you must be a friend to make a friend. It wasn't done by Derrick keeping the ball as he had before, but by giving it up.

Identification

Did you ever wonder why gangs always wear the same colors? It's the same reason a soccer team wears the same uniform: identifi-cation. The shirt, shorts, and knee-highs are all it takes to make them part of the team. The difference is, of course, you want your child to be part of the soccer team, not part of a gang.

At around age nine, children begin to want to dress like their peers rather than their parents. It's the beginning of peer identification, when kids start to form their own ideas and their own identity. It's critical for them to learn how to relate to their peers, to give and take, and to identify with other children. But it's important for parents to ensure their child's first colors are team colors.

Community Walls

Our soccer district encompassed both the east and west sides of town. The east contained the poor neighborhoods, many immigrant families from Central America, families on welfare, street gangs. The west was a world away, very affluent, home to middle-class professionals, doctors, lawyers, movie producers, and the like.

The first soccer practice I held reflected the same divisions that separated those communities. On the south touchline were the Hispanic parents from the east. Huddled along the north touchline were the affluent parents from the west. The two African American parents stood on their own behind one of the goals. The kids separated themselves into two teams along exactly the same lines.

Walls Come Tumbling Down

By the time we played our first game, the stands still reflected the same ethnic and financial differences, but out on the field, the kids were separated only by position. There were defenders, forwards, and midfielders; kids with blue eyes and blond hair, brown eyes and black hair; kids with pale skin, kids with brown or black skin; there were good players and not-so-good players. But there was no difference in their enthusiasm for the game or the sense of fun and excitement each of them had.

They worked as a team. They respected and counted upon one another. They were an example to their parents. By mid-season, I took a moment to survey the touchlines once more. A miracle had occurred. The divisions had disappeared. Families from the east sat with those from the west. The two communities mingled as one, joined by the common bond of supporting their kids' soccer team. When the team won they cheered as one; when the team lost, they consoled each other's kids.

They had been brought together by a simple game. Soccer was the only uniform that they or their kids needed.

From the Doctor's Desk

Soccer provides the "uniform," the sense of belonging to a team that kids need. At the same time, it teaches them to respect one another, to act responsibly, and develops a set of values.

At this age there are no "rotten apples," only those who have been left to stew in front of a TV or with the wrong bunch. Soccer is the pie that binds the apples together. Children who live by the rules of soccer are taught respect, are not easily bored, and are less likely to succumb to the lure of gangs.

25

The Family Value

The 25th Life Lesson:
Recognize When a Good Thing Is Too Much

Mary and Ed

"I don't understand it, Doctor, my husband has the same values as I do, he is responsible, caring, diligent, and honest, but we just don't seem ever to be together." A tear fell off Mary's cheek. "We barely see one another on weekends, during the week he works late. I say more to the grocery clerk than to him. I am worried about our marriage, the kids, everything." Calmly I said, "You do have your two daughters in my daughter's soccer league." I knew Mary to be an extremely dedicated mother. "I see you there often. What about Ed, how come he doesn't come down to the games with you, he's not working is he?"

"No," Mary said. "He takes my two sons camping and hunting. He is a great father, but our household seems to be in two separate camps. I'm at the soccer field, he's lost in the forest with my sons."

The Family Family Value

In my practice there is one family value that causes more problems than any other. It is a family value that is inherited, or rather, learned. Simply put, it is what your family likes to do, what your family thinks is important. Some families love to go to the movies, others do sports, and some pursue intellectual hobbies. We bring these interests with us to our marriage. We often take it for granted that everyone values and likes the same ideas and activities with which we were brought up. We never doubt this until we get married.

Mary came from a family that cherished sports. Her memories were set on baseball diamonds, in football arenas, and on soccer fields. Her family valued athletic prowess and in fact whenever they gathered the topic of discussion always began with the latest sports headlines. It was a common bond that all her family shared. When she had children they would play ball.

Then she married Ed.

Ed was raised on a ranch in Texas. He was going to make sure his sons could "rough it" and take care of themselves in any situation. When he had children they were going to hunt and camp. His family did that on their vacations. That's how *they* bonded.

A wonderful family. Two good people. But they stand divided because they have different values and ideas about fun. They each feel their child or children must have the same activities in their life because *their* nuclear family valued these pursuits so dearly.

These family values or hobbies can either strengthen or destroy a family, unless they are recognized and discussed.

Resolution

If you find yourself alone at the soccer field when your wife or husband could be there, sit down and talk. Family unity is quickly becoming extinct, but that can be changed if the parents compromise. I gave Mary some homework. Her daughters love soccer and softball and were good. They were not into "killing animals and roughing it." I knew this was not going to be easy.

But Mary and Ed did it. During the soccer season the boys joined the soccer league so that Mary and Ed could participate in their kids' extracurricular activities together, going from the girls' field to the boys' field hand in hand. In the summer they all went camping. Ed agreed to leave the guns home!

Too Much

I was in a full sprint down the corridor, threw open the garage door, jumped into my Volkswagen, and tore out of the driveway. I sped by my neighbor who was taking his family to church. I had to pick up Vinnie from his tennis lesson to get him to the soccer practice on time. After all, I was an assistant coach, and God knows how I had drummed into the parents how important it was to be on time. As I sped down the street, I could hear the Sunday church bells chiming. You might ask, where was my wife? Well, she was across town with my son Mikey at his basketball game. It was early September, not even noon on a Sunday, and I had been driving and racing from one sporting event to another with my wife doing the same in a second car. What do people do when they have only one car?

That night I sat down with my wife and we realized that

since March, the beginning of the baseball season, we had not spent one weekend away as a family and with the onset of soccer season that might extend into December. Among our three kids we were involved in soccer, tennis, baseball, karate, piano, guitar, and to end it all with a bang, drum lessons for Mikey. Yes, our children even went to school, I think, for a rest! Both my wife and I valued sports: She had been a national karate champion and I enjoyed all types of sports. But when is a good thing too much of a good thing?

When the Family Stops Growing

It was clear to me that since all of our children were in multiple sports, rarely did they have time to watch or support one another. The activities were often on the same day, and when I got home from work, there was barely time to eat dinner together, no less talk to one another. My wife and I collapsed on the same bed at night; otherwise, we might never meet. Our children, at times, had to be dragged to their activities, when they should have wanted to go. Taking Kaycee to piano lessons and Vinnie to guitar lessons was like making them eat spinach. Mikey, however, enjoyed banging those drums. I let my wife taken him there; my brain couldn't take it.

The good rules of thumb that things are getting out of control are:

1. When you tell your children it is time for dinner, they say, "I want a number-two supersized."
2. The only time the family is really together is when you are all in bed.

3. When you all stop smiling and start using words like "you must, you should, you have to," instead of "I want, I can't wait, let's all go."

Then you know the family is not growing together, but rather growing in parallel universes. Then you must make a change.

From the Doctor's Desk

A family value is an interest or pursuit your particular family cherishes. There are sports families, movie-buff families, outdoor families, musical families, and so on.

Parents must discuss in each particular case:

1. What their family of origin's particular interest was.
2. How strongly they feel that their child pursue this.
3. Compromise is a must if there is a disagreement between parents.
4. If you disagree as to the value of some family interest, such as having a couple of drinks after dinner versus going to a ball game together or praying as a family, answer these questions:

   • Which will increase your child's physical, emotional, spiritual, and intellectual health most?
   • Ten years from now, which will prepare your child for a career or marriage?
   • Twenty years from now, would you like them to pass these values on to their children?
   • Which will best develop their character, conscience, and courage?

If you still can't decide, do your best to compromise. Saying, "I won't stop you from doing your thing with the children" is as good as being a hindrance.

To build a family value or interest it takes everyone's involvement and compromise.

Remember, compromise your interests and pursuits, but never compromise your principles of character and conscience. If you go camping or play soccer it is altogether a different thing. It is a family interest.

Remember

1. Remember when entering your child into soccer, be certain both you and your husband are in agreement and realize it is a commitment.
2. Remember soccer is more than a commitment. It is an opportunity to be together, to laugh, to have fun, to grow, to bond as a family.
3. Remember if you feel alone in your commitment, sit down and discuss how you might compromise.

Once again, the family that kicks together seasonally, sticks together reasonably.

PART VI

COACHING

Being a coach is like being a parent and sibling to your team, a friend to all. It requires a person with a dream that everyone can and will have fun; someone with eternal hope, no matter how hard the going gets; a person with faith in both himself and his children.

A great coach is an inspiration to all those around him. To be a great coach takes a good heart, determination, and a sense of humor.

As the coach you have the power to:
make a child laugh or cry,
make a child quit or try,
inspire hope or the feeling that all is lost,
win with honor or at all cost,
harm or cure,
make a child feel secure or unsure,
show courage or cowardice,
encourage or inhibit,
show humor or anger,
play honorably or unfairly.

As the soccer season comes to close at winter,
You the coach have the power to even lose but be a winner.

As a coach you can touch a child's life and be the difference. I've seen it done.

26

The Coach

The 26th Life Lesson:
He Who Has Fire, Warms Others

Knowing *why* you are a coach may be different from *what* you expect from being a coach.

The Moment of Truth

This was it. My entire career as a soccer coach had come down to this single crucial moment. The glittering World Cup beckoned. The U.S. national team was just moments away from a historic victory over Brazil in the World Cup Final.

I knew I had to be patient, hope we could hold on to the one-goal lead. If we could just survive this last-minute free kick, we'd surely be there. But as I shouted orders from the touchline, in the back of my mind I was already writing glorious headlines like "Fabulous Fortanasce Captures the Cup!"

Suddenly I felt a tug on my shorts and opened my eyes. Little

Geralyn had abandoned her position in defense to walk over to me. "Coach, I gotta go to the bathroom," she said, and with that my dreams of World Cup glory were dashed.

But was the dream of glory the reason I became a soccer coach? Of course I wanted to help kids, or maybe just help my own kids— no coach was going to bench my children unless it was me. When I recall why I first starting coaching, I realize I had several agendas. The conscious motivation was to be a good influence, inspire kids, make a difference maybe. I think I also wanted to protect my own kids from some of the lunatic coaches I'd seen. But deep down in my unconscious, the motivation to become a coach lay in a single baseball pitch I made some forty years ago.

It was the last inning of the Little League play-offs. I had just blown two pitches past the batter and now figured I'd surprise him with a change-up, a meatball, a triple off the fence. He became the hero, condemning me to game-losing goat, the person who loses for the whole team. How could I have made such a stupid decision?

No, I hardly remember that horrific day at all. Not me. Not Vince Fortanasce, M.D. I didn't need glory and adulation. As you can tell, my unconscious motivation, my unconscious expectation was to dull that memory by becoming a winning coach, the hero that I had failed to be forty years ago.

My unconscious expectations are clear and a possible detriment to the children under me. Once I became aware of this I had a better chance to be a coach there for the children.

Myra

It was my third season. Myra was only one of three players I had a chance to pick in the draft. It seemed she was literally dragged out to the soccer field by her mother. I had selected her because the previous year I had noticed she was an accomplished player and her mother was very supportive and attended every game. A team with parental support is always a good team, win or lose.

I went over to Myra to find out what was wrong. Drawing on my background as a psychiatrist, I probed for the cause of her reluctance using an obsequious innuendo. "How are you, Myra? Nice to have you on my team." Myra just gave me a suspicious stare and trudged off to the sideline.

I decided I needed a slightly more direct approach. "You seem sad," I said. Identifying a child's feelings gives her the opportunity to validate and explain it.

"I'm not sad," she replied curtly, "I'm mad."

Ah, the opening I needed for a frontal attack. "Mad?" I asked gently. By repeating the last word of someone's sentence, it opens the door for continued discussion, a door I should have left shut.

"I don't like soccer and I don't like you," she said with venom. "Last year, you said they shouldn't kick the ball to my side because I was weak and slow like a 'beached whale.' And you and the other coaches don't want me, you just want my mom because she's so pretty!"

What? What! She said I called her a "beached whale?" I gulped guiltily. Gee, I have often thought of using that term—and several other less-than-flattering terms to describe some of the weaker players—but did I really utter them? I guess I had. I certainly never directed it at Myra—she was an excellent player—but just imagine what I had done to the child I had really aimed that remark at. What, I thought, made me say such things? How insensitive, how stupid.

As a coach you can heal or you can harm. A year later, Myra still nursed the wound from a misdirected barb. As for Myra's mother, I can assure you all, while other coaches may be influenced by a pretty face, I certainly was not.

What Is the Coach?

As the coach, you are the doctor, the janitor, and the role model for kids and parents. An AYSO survey found that the chief reason that 70 percent of youngsters returned for another season of youth soccer was because of their coach. If was also the chief reason why they didn't return. The coach's position is pivotal. He is the captain of the ship and defines the priorities of the game.

Expectations

Like parents, the coach must be in touch with his own expectations. It's crucial to making the soccer field a healthy, harmonious environment for children to learn and grow. Unlike parents, however, a coach must also be in touch with the expectations of all his players and their parents and stepparents, siblings, and other relatives who attend practices and games. This of course is not to mention the expectations of the opposing team's three or four coaches, players, parents, and so on.

Expectations do influence the coach and it is his unconscious expectations that can land him in hot water with his team's parents, the other team's parents, the other team's coach, or all at once. It's enough to bring any sane person to the boiling point. The season hasn't even begun, but the coach is already dealing with a flood of conflicting expectations from soccer moms and dads. It can test the mettle of even a gentle, easygoing coach. It can bring a competitive one to the brink.

The secret to surviving as a coach is to keep your focus, keep your objectives clear, and establish early on exactly what you will and won't tolerate in the season to come. This should be laid out at the team's first meeting—what I call *The Mother of All Meetings* (see Chapter 27). But before going on, do you know what a coach's objectives should be? It helps to focus on the following whenever you see a parent or have a quiet moment alone with him or her.

1. Establish that the soccer field is there for the kids to play and have fun.
2. Parents must be reminded to keep the game in perspective— it's a game, not a life-and-death struggle.
3. Remind yourself that developing talent (physical prowess) is secondary to developing a child's conscience and character.
4. A coach must always insist on what is right for the children, not *who* is right.
5. A coach must listen, and learn to be a mentor to the kids and a mediator to their parents.
6. Remember, at all times you are the example; be all you can be; be the best example of a leader, father or mother, under-standing but assertive, kind but firm.

Positive Coaching

Louie

Louie was an experienced coach who'd played soccer all his life and was known for his highly organized and well-disciplined teams. As a rookie coach, I once sat in on one of his practice sessions to get some general tips on training techniques. But unexpectedly, I learned something much more important than teaching kids skills. I discovered how to infuse them with so much spirit that they were excited to play.

"Kim, great tackle!" Louie roared to one of his young defenders. "You maintained your balance and kept your eye on the ball rather than committing yourself to Jim's fake. Excellent." He clapped his hands and gave Kim a thumbs up, his smile nearly as broad as the little nine-year-old's.

When his players seemed to tire in the humid evening, he began a well-practiced chant. "Who are we?" he yelled. "The Hornets!" they shouted back. "Who?" he says louder. They shouted back more enthusiastically, "The Hornets!"

"And what are we gonna do?"

"Buzz!! Swarm!!" the kids shouted in unison and started to make a buzzing sound and shake their fingers in the air. They were suddenly filled with a renewed energy. It seemed Louie had a chant for every position on the team. The defenders did the "Hornet Shuffle": They took a step forward, one left, one right, and then back, all the while buzzing loudly. Louie's techniques injected enthusiasm into the players and proved infectious to the spectators. I couldn't help smiling and winking at my daughter as she shuffled and buzzed around the field. Parents were as much a part of the rituals of this team as their children. The kids were having fun and no parent here was allowed to sit back and chat on a cell phone.

Thanks to the coach.

Do As Lou!

The attitude of the coach is all important. Louie never lost sight of the fact that the children were there to have fun. His philosophy was "Always look for the positives."

1. Keep a five-to-one ratio of praise to criticism. Remember: Praise in public, criticize in private.
2. Catch a child doing well.
3. Praise with specifics. "Great tackle, well controlled, excellent pass."
4. Praise with animation. "Wow, that was something else."
5. Notice progress and tell the child what you see. For example, notice frequency: when a player makes more tackles, or an older player (fifteen and above) makes more headers. Notice intensity: trying harder, determined to be involved in the game. Notice duration: running longer, faster.
6. Laugh a lot, invent games like the Hornet Shuffle that are private to your team and make them feel part of something unique.
7. Remember player safety. Seventy percent of injuries are considered avoidable by coaches if they have players warm up correctly. Teach the proper technique for heading a ball and discourage high kicks and dangerous tackles.
8. Be persistent. How to behave in the good, right, and fair way can never be repeated enough.
9. Be concrete. Tell them, show them, no matter how simple it seems.
10. Be consistent. Treat every player the same, every day. Don't let your emotions, the stresses at work, cause your attitude, your behavior to vary day by day. Let your kids' behavior be their destiny, not yours.

11. Remember the age of your children and teach them accordingly. Five- to nine-year-olds need simple, one-stage commands. Show them, tell them, and make them do the drills. Practices should be short, using visual, auditory, and kinesthetic examples. Ten- to twelve-year-olds need more complex commands, longer practice, thirty to sixty minutes. Input for teaching should be positive and supportive.
12. Never lose the opportunity to be an example of honesty, fairness, character, and courage.
13. Remember, there is no victory without honor.

Motivation

Motivation is the key to being a successful coach. Motivation induces behavior that is beneficial to the child and the team. Kids are motivated when they are having fun, learning new skills, and getting positive support from their coach.

Motivation comes from within. You, the coach, are the motivator, the cheerleader, and your enthusiasm can be infectious, lighting up your players. Children are motivated when they are having fun, when their coach is happy and when their parents are happy. In this kind of atmosphere children are most willing and able to learn. In this kind of atmosphere the character principles of camaraderie, loyalty, honesty, respect, and gratitude blossom. After all, I've never heard of a coach who consistently bent the rules, taught his players to cheat and deceive the referee, who was also smiling, enthusiastic, and kind!

It's important for each coach and each parent to assess his own mood. Chances are, if you're happy and smiling, you're teaching honesty and fair play. If you're frowning and angry, it brings out the worst elements in the game. Leave your troubles at work, or at home. Be happy. Smile. Laugh. All it takes is a decision.

Why Laugh?

Physiologically, laughter increases endorphins and serotonin, which reduces stress, relaxes the body, and allows the central (enjoyment) area of the brain to take over. This in turn increases creativity and activity in the neocortex or thinking brain, which induces you to do and say things to enhance and continue the feelings of well-being.

Most important, laughter is infectious. It brings kids back and allows parents to laugh at themselves, reducing confrontations. As we've said before, it's harder for the opposing coach and players to want to beat someone who is having fun, someone they like.

Laughter Is the Winner

The legendary Argentine player Diego Maradonna, was considered the best player in the world during the 1980s, capable of winning any game with a sudden flash of unstoppable brilliance. He was, however, also noted for his intensity. The angrier, more intense he was, the better he played. For a World Cup qualifying game against Peru, the Peruvian coach decided to get his most engaging and funniest player to mark Maradonna. During the game, he constantly told short jokes and anecdotes to the Argentine. Maradonna's intensity waned and he played without his usual fervor. With Maradonna playing below par, Peru pulled off an upset and won the game. This is an excellent example of both the power of laughter, emotional intelligence, and *positive* gamesmanship.

In youth soccer, children win (by having a good time and building character) when coaches make the game as fun as possible. In doing so, they also set a great example to the kids: they keep the game and the result in perspective and treat everyone with a smile. Remember, one minute of laughter is worth more than ten minutes of shouting.

Lou the Leader

Soccer is supposed to be fun, but if you've been a soccer parent, sometimes it is painful. I remember well my first season as a child when I sat on the bench. Everyone else was out on the field playing. Just another boy and I sat alone on the bench. I mean really alone. I sat with both hands clasped under my cheeks, my elbows resting on my knees like Rodin's *Thinker,* but instead, I was *The Sulker.* I was left out. My dad sadly watched me from the bleachers. I was being left out. Yes it was only for half the game, but it was also telling me I'm the worst.

I've seen that same dejected look on many kids in my experience in youth sports. Not only those who are left out for half a game but the others who want to be a striker instead of a midfielder, a goalkeeper instead of a defender. It always seemed that no matter what you did as a coach, you couldn't be everything to everybody. Then one day I saw Lou coach. "Coach, I don't want to play in defense anymore," said Tommy. "Why can't I play forward? I'm just as good." From what I'd seen of

Tommy I knew he wasn't as talented in front of the goal as Lou's current forwards. I wondered what a coach says to a player like Tommy. Maybe something like, "Look, slowpoke, don't kid yourself."

Lou bent down so he was eye level with Tommy and said, "Tommy, how many wheels are on your dad's car?" Tommy told him there were four. "And is there any one wheel," continued Lou, "that is more important than the others?" Without waiting for an answer, Lou said, "No, the car can't go without all four wheels working. Our team is like a car. You are one of the wheels. Without you in defense, the team can't go. Remember, every position on the team is just as important as the others. If the other team can't score, can they win?" Tommy shook his head. "Well," Lou went on, "if you stop them from scoring, you are the reason for our success. Tommy's eyes brightened and he ran back to his position with a renewed look of determination on his face.

Lou had a similar speech for every position on the team. He called his midfielders "the magicians." They created the plays, but when the team is under attack they become defenders and when the team is attacking they magically turn into forwards. They are the planners, the thinkers, who set up the forwards. For the forwards, he taught them responsibility. When they scored, they had to run back and thank the rest of the players for their help.

Lou created teamwork. Each child knew how important his position was. At the end of every game, he gave awards to a midfielder, a forward, and a defender or the goalkeeper, who was nicknamed "The Big Cat" because of the way he pounced on the ball. Lou also had some great advice for parents who, like 90 percent of Americans, knew little or nothing about soccer and often couldn't understand why their child couldn't play in the "glory positions."

Lou gave the same advice regarding soccer positions to the parents. For example, to illustrate the importance of defenders he would talk about the Italian men's national soccer team, which has always been built around a strong defense, has won three World Cups, and is always in contention at major tournaments. The record transfer fee for a player in the English Premier League, one of the top leagues in the world, was for a defender.

But what Lou taught most to parents was to understand the temperament and athletic abilities of their children. If your child is aggressive and fast, he may well do well as a striker. The attentive child, who can read the game well, plan, and has a lot of soccer skill may make a good midfielder. The reliable, steady, well-disciplined child may be best suited as a defender. The goalkeepers, like basketball players, are usually the children who are tall, agile, and good with their hands.

Remember, whatever position your child plays, it is an important position, as he is part of a team. However, if you let him know directly or indirectly that you're disappointed about where he plays, you may be responsible for his dissatisfaction. Your dissatisfaction means to your child that:

1. You are not proud of him.
2. He is a victim or is being deliberately left out.

This causes dissension and a loss of team cohesion and results in bickering. The opportunity to teach team loyalty and cooperation is lost. Most important is the need for a child to be content with himself. If he is, no matter what his position, he will feel self-satisfied and self-confident, attributes he'll keep as he grows up.

From the Doctor's Desk

The secret of a great coach is that he knows he is there not for himself or for the parents, but for the children. You don't have to be a doctor, child psychologist, or successful business executive to be a successful coach. All you need is common sense, an infectious enthusiasm for the game and a determination to be the best example you can be to the children.

A C-O-A-C-H is:

C: Character. An example of honesty, responsibility, and respect.

O: Organized. Responsible for giving each player and parent a well-defined role within the team.

A: Attitude. Uses five positive remarks for every negative one.

C: Courageous enough to stand up for what is best for the kids.

H: Honorable to players, parents, referees, and especially opponents.

How to be a great coach involves A-T-T-I-T-U-D-E:

A: Affable. Be friendly, smile, laugh.

T: Treat children equally and fairly.

T: Treat parents fairly.

I: Invent new means of teaching and leading.

T: Tolerate and be sensitive to parents and coaches, and referees.

U: Use all parents' and children's gifts.

D: Develop and reward their efforts.

E: Energize. People with fire warm others. Be the inspiration.

27

The Mother of All Meetings

The 27th Life Lesson:
The First Meeting Is the Mother of All Meetings

I was late for the first parent-coach meeting of the season and if Hank started the meeting before I got there the season would effectively be over, because he was such a bully.

As I finally pulled up the driveway, I scanned the parked cars for Hank's red Firebird. I couldn't see it. Thank you, God. Hank was running late as well. I was there before him. The season was saved.

I entered the room and greeted the parents—nearly all of them were there, some were even exuding enthusiasm, the rest were anxiously tapping their watches, keen to remind me that *Monday Night Football* started in forty minutes.

I'd learned from my experience as a coach that the "meat" of the meeting was not a rundown of the rules or team schedule but establishing why the parents were there and to discuss their expectations of youth soccer. As a professor of medical students, I knew that students had a 25 percent chance of remembering anything you taught. If you asked them a question that they answered correctly, their recall rate was raised to 50 percent. If they answered incorrectly, however, the recall rate was up to 77 percent.

The Test

My first topic was priorities. How important, relative to, say, their house or their car, is their child?

Second question: What do you want your child to get out of soccer?

A few hands went up immediately. I ignored those parents, and hunted out one avoiding my gaze. I spotted shy Mr. Gump doing his best to hide behind the ample figure of Mrs. Gallagher. Those without a patterned answer usually give the best picture of the genuine underlying expectations of the group. "Mr. Gump, what do you think?"

"I guess," he responded slowly, "to learn how to win, to be competitive." I turned to two other parents who hadn't raised their hands and they agreed. "To win," each replied, with growing confidence each time.

I repeated their answer in different words. "So you want your children to beat other children?" I asked. "What if they don't and they are beaten?"

Some of the parents were growing uneasy now, averting their eyes, squirming in their seats. I paused, then turned to one mother whose arm was flapping in the air like a schoolgirl's. "To have fun, to learn how to get along, and to learn new skills," she stated proudly.

I never respond with an immediate "correct" or "that's

right," but always pause. The few moments of suspense gives people time to think about what's been said and increases the likelihood they'll remember it. Finally, I nodded and said, "Yes. The reason I coach this team is for the children to have fun, learn new skills, and, most important, to build character, conscience, and courage—the three Cs."

How?

How can we teach the three Cs? I tell parents, "The primary responsibility is yours. It starts at home and continues through the opportunities that the game of soccer provides. Coaches and referees are important, but not as important as you, the parents."

I will then illustrate situations that often occur with soccer and make suggestions as to how they should handle each. For example:

Situation one: Another parent on the other side starts taunting your children. What should you do?

Suggestion: Notify your coach, who can ask the referee to take action. Applaud the opposing team when they make a good play. This often embarrasses the berating parent and sends a clear message about your ideals of sportsmanship. As a coach, it is important to ask your parents to shake hands with the parents of the opposing team before the game.

Situation two: You feel your child is not being given a fair chance at playing.

Suggestion: Encourage your child to talk to you about it, remembering that her position on the team is not as important as your clear satisfaction and acceptance of her.

Situation three: Your child has just made a deliberate, illegal tackle. How do you tell your child why it was wrong?

Suggestion: The answer is not "because you were penalized." Remind him of the spirit behind the rules, and the Golden Rule of soccer and of life: Don't do something to someone else that you wouldn't want done to you.

Situation four: Another player elbows your child at every corner kick-in order to get a better position. How do you tell your child to deal with it? "Elbow back so he has your respect"?

Suggestion: Tell him two wrongs don't make a right. Notify the coach and the referee. Cheating shouldn't be tolerated. Remember, the difference between courage and confrontation. If angry, don't confront, just walk away or ask me, your coach, to intervene.

Situation five: Your child is playing badly. Should you praise him or her?

Suggestion: Always emphasize the positive. Even if he's playing badly, praise his effort, his determination. Don't just praise the good players—they are all one team and deserve praise together.

Situation six: Your team is losing. Is this a reason to cheer?

Suggestion: Cheering and enthusiasm are especially needed when a team is down. Kids need it the most when they seem to deserve it the least. Remember, kids only believe the score is important if you tell them it is. This works well with children under nine. Use the adage: "Try and try harder. Never give up!"

Situation seven: After a game that you couldn't attend, what do you ask your child?

Suggestion: Never ask: "Did you win?" Instead try: "Did

254 🏈 LIFE LESSONS FROM SOCCER

you have a good time?" or, "What did you do?" which will give
your child the opportunity to be appreciated.

Responsibility

At the parents' meeting, I remind them of the following responsibilities:

Enrolling their child into soccer is a commitment for them
as well as their child. They have a responsibility to be present at
as many games as possible, at least 50 percent of them. Parents
should seize the opportunities that each game and practice session offer to bond with their child. They are responsible for the
following:

1. Ensuring that their child arrives at games and practice ses-
    sions on time and with the correct equipment.
2. Reiterating the principles of character, conscience, and
    courage.
3. Helping their child to accept defeat graciously.
4. Rewarding their children for honesty, trustworthiness, and
    loyalty to the team and acknowledging when they fall short
    of these ideals.

In ten years, none of the kids will remember the score of
these games, who won or lost. But the memories of the fun they
had and the sense of honesty and loyalty they developed will
stay with them forever.

I also reminded parents that they should:

1. Never compare their child with another.

2. Never scold their child in front of his or her friends.
3. Always look for signs of a problem through the child's non-verbal signals.

Preparation

1. Place the season's soccer schedule in a place where both you and your child can see it on a daily basis.
2. Wash the uniform prior to game day.
3. Put the kid's soccer kit—shoes, shirt, shin guards, ball, etc.—in the same place after each game, so you'll know where to find it next time. This reduces the most common stress associated with preparation before a game: not finding equipment. Kids ten years and older should take responsibility for this preparation.

The Coach

To round off the meeting, I make a point of reiterating the fact that I am a volunteer who coaches the kids for the sheer joy of it. "I am not perfect and I have never been a professional coach or player. But I am caring and am concerned about the well-being of each child on my team. And I do need your support. Especially when the team is losing." After all, coaches need parental support when they seem to deserve it the least, too!

From the Doctor's Desk

The tone, the tempo, the eventual outcome of the season starts with the Mother of All Meetings. The keys outlined in Section 1 are crucial to a coach.

Presence: It is most important to have all parents present at the meeting. Stress the protocols and the importance that parents attend all games.

Communication: Let the parents know they can talk to you. If it's something important concerning their child, ask them to make a written note to remind you. Parents tend to approach a coach when he is distracted or often don't impress the importance of what they wish to say.

Acceptance: A coach must make each child feel special and remember the sign that each child wears: "Make me feel important."

28

The Coach's Letter

The 28th Life Lesson:
Lay It All Down on Paper

I remember my first Mother of All Meetings like I remember my first toothache. I never knew it could be so painful. Before the meeting, I'd sent out a short letter outlining my philosophy, objectives, coaching methods, and what I as the coach expected from the parents, as well as, of course, a note on schedule and equipment.

I later found out that only two parents had read the letter. The rest just noted the date and place of the meeting and tossed the letter. My subsequent letters were learning experiences.

The second year I wrote *It is mandatory for all parents to read this letter* in bold letters at the top of the page. In year three, I learned a fresh lesson, and wrote the message on the *outside* of the envelope, *Mandatory reading, please open!* It seems many parents had to be encouraged to open the envelope let alone read the contents. I was no different in my first season as a parent in Little League. I never read anything I was given. I was too busy and too important. After all, how much could there be to know about a kid's sport?

The Letter

In addition to noting the date and location of the first meeting, as well as any details about equipment required and a schedule of games and practices, I recommend including the following:

Dear Parents,

Welcome to soccer, one of the first steps in your child's development. My objectives as your child's coach are to build the three Cs:

Character: To demonstrate, through my example, the meaning of honesty, responsibility, loyalty, and discipline.

Conscience: To help build your child's sense of right and wrong.

Courage: To stand up for their conscience, to stand up for what is right. To take responsibility when something goes wrong and to never be afraid to say, "I made a mistake."

To do this, I need each parent to:

1.   Be present at games as much as possible. It is the greatest gift you can give your child.

2.   Understand your child is not an adult physically, emotionally, or intellectually and grows bit by bit.

3.   Have a positive attitude. Praise your child's efforts, not the results. Have five positive comments for every negative one.

4. *Be* consistent. *Let your words and actions send the same message throughout the season.*

5. Accept *your child for the gifts given him or her. Don't make your child responsible for your happiness. Don't worry if your child is not a great player, only if he or she is a happy, contented player.*

Remember, on my team winning is not the priority, building the three Cs—Character, Conscience and Courage—is. Building ability is secondary to building an honest, responsible, and contented child.

I can't do this without your help.

Signed:

Your Coach

P.S. Don't be afraid to remind me what I said in this letter at any point during the coming season!

29

The Marathon

The 29th Life Lesson:
Life Is a Marathon, Not a Series of Hundred-Yard
Dashes

It's All Small Stuff

Carlos was a talented ten-year-old, with the ball at his feet and
his father on his back. His father was constantly shouting out
suggestions from the sideline. The intensity of his voice and the
anguish etched upon his face would make one think that the
entire world and his son's future existence rested upon the next
pass or the next shot on goal. Carlos's dad was a classic example
of the "unfulfilled" parent.

Watching Carlos practice, I overheard the recriminations
from his dad. "You'll never make it," he said. "You don't try
hard enough." Then, "You need to be faster, stronger." His
words were spoken with the intensity of a ringside trainer to a

heavyweight boxer vying for the world championship before the eyes of millions. All Carlos could reply was, "I'm sorry, Dad. I'll do it for you, Dad."

Some people fail to see that soccer, kindergarten, high school, and college are single milestones in a child's life. It is not one game, one season, nor even soccer itself that is going to determine a child's eventual success. The long-term goals of child development far outweigh the short-term wins racked up on the scoreboard. Victory is bringing children back again for another season.

What Is Planted in Players
Is Better Than What Is Poured on Them

Carlos's dad did not recognize that life is a marathon. Each goal scored, each pass missed, is rather meaningless when put into perspective of a child's entire life. When he was a grown man, would Carlos remember a missed shot? Only if his father made it painful enough for him. A parent's lack of perspective affects a child's feelings of self-worth.

The Journey's Destination

One of the chief reasons why parents and coaches often fail in their quest to be all they can be for their children is because of their lack of perspective.

Many adults believe that their job hangs on every decision they make at work. While this is unlikely, these same people often carry that perspective in to their home lives and onto the soccer field.

These parents and coaches place such significance on each season, each game, and even on each pass. As I mentioned before, if winning is a parent's or coach's definition of success, it will doom their children and the team to eventual failure. Often, by the time she gets to the game a parent or coach has been working all day, is tense, stressed-out, and therefore tends to lose perspective about why she's there. Remember: This is just one step in a child's life, albeit an important step. It is a time when the child can learn self-acceptance and the principles of character *if* the parents and coaches can maintain *their* perspective. It is the teaching of life lessons that is the truly important aspect of a soccer game. Not a bad pass, a sloppy tackle, or a missed shot.

The eventual goal of youth soccer is not to rack up more goals than the other team, but to develop self-confidence and self-esteem within a child. This is not taught by one pass, one game, or one season. It is taught by fostering the building blocks of character and morality that are built morsel by morsel over many seasons. It's the journey's end.

Coaching the Marathon

To coach for the long term rather than the short term, coaches need to:

1. Teach parents the importance of losing today but winning tomorrow.
2. Overcome the short-term attitudes of parents by emphasizing long-term goals.
3. Balance winning a game versus building a team.

Some coaches with initially winning teams lose in the end. Others with mediocre teams finish strongly. Why? The answer is simple. Some coaches are coaching for a single game, a single season even. Others are coaching for the marathon. These are the coaches with fire, who warm and kindle effort. Remember, effort breeds success.

 From the Doctor's Desk

Coaches and parents:

1. Keep perspective of the child's journey.
2. Remember, life is long—childhood is short.
3. Before reacting, stop and think, how will this affect the child's character and sense of right and wrong?
4. When making a decision, think, how will this affect the child tomorrow? Ten years from now? Then act accordingly.
5. Keep a sense of humor.
6. Encourage a child's hopes and dreams, reduce his anxieties and fears by being calm and smiling.
7. Remember you are there for the children, they are not there for you.

The single best piece of advice I can give coaches comes from the words of Thomas Jefferson: "In matters of style, swim with the current. In matters of principle, stand like a rock."

30

How to Find the Right Coach

The 30th Life Lesson:
The Best Coach Is the "Vowel-uable" Coach

A soccer coach may be a major role model to your child. The average coach spends six hours a week with his team, often more time than a parent spends directly supervising her child. Therefore, it is vital that parents choose the right coach.

The year after Hank coached the Bears, we lost 40 percent of the children from the previous season. The kids had not moved out of town, been eaten by space invaders, or even joined gangs or developed drug habits. They and their parents had just had a bad experience with Hank. His "win-at-all-costs" attitude, rule bending, and general unsportsmanlike behavior had taken its toll. Referees hated officiating his games, since he would invariably run out onto the field to disagree with a call and other coaches. Hank's players had, inevitably, adopted his poor attitude and confrontational demeanor. They would berate the referee when a call went against them, calling him "four eyes" or "blind as a bat." They were renowned throughout the league for their late, rough, and often dangerous tackling. The Bears were also famous for feigning injury and making dramatic dives in the box looking for penalties, all improper and unethical soccer techniques encouraged by Hank.

Some of the other coaches decided that if they could not beat Hank, they'd join him, so every game involved at least one major confrontation. Soccer was not a game anymore, it was a hard, bitter lesson in the dog-eat-dog realities of life on the battlefield. At times, the Bears' game looked more like the floor of the New York Stock Exchange or divorce court than a kids' soccer contest.

This was not just my imagination. The telltale signs spoke volumes. Parent participation dwindled, coaches—even those on his own team—arrived late, and the players seemed to derive less and less enjoyment from each game.

If a bad coach can have such a devastating effect on a team, it's important to know the characteristics of a good coach.

The Characteristics of a Good Coach

What should you look for in a coach? The basic characteristics of a good coach are found in the "vowel-uable" coach. Look for a coach with the right A-E-I-O-U (and F):

A for Attitude: Which goes with a positive regard and loving encouragement. These are the "good-play" and "nice-try" with-a-smile coaches, the ones that turn an error into an opportunity to learn.

E for Enthusiasm: Coaches with a spirit that captures both children and parents. The "high-five" and "2-4-6-8-who-do-we-appreciate" coach who welcomes everyone with a smile and a handshake.

I for Integrity: The coach whose principles encourage cooperation and mutual responsibility, the coach who wins even when he loses. He is the coach you hope your child grows up to be like.

O for Objective: The coach who indicates why he wanted the job and what he expects children and parents to get out of his coaching. He puts winning games second, teamwork and spirit first. The "what-is-best-for-the-kids" coach.

U for Understanding: A good coach listens at eye level and understands the needs of both children and parents. He understands the need for him to be reliable, considerate, and always follow through with his promises. His words are, "How is your child doing?" and, "How are you doing?"

F for Fundamentals: Someone who understands the basics of soccer.

Women are often the best coaches because of their sensitivity and knowledge of children's needs and development.

One knows her child has a good coach by the enthusiasm on the player's face when he walks in the door from practice.

How to Find That Coach

Finding the right coach for your child is the key to his or her enjoyment of soccer. Start by calling the regional commissioner or the organization's head office, whether it be the AYSO (800-USA-AYSO), or any other youth soccer group. AYSO will put you in contact with one of their 1,000 regional headquarters, and if there isn't one near you, AYSO can assist you in setting one up. Youth soccer officials hear all the complaints of parents and usually know who they would like to coach their own kids. Give a lot of consideration to their recommendations.

Second, ask parents who have children in the same soccer league. Never feel you are imposing when you call a stranger about your child. Just think of the rewarding experience you may be giving him or her.

Unfortunately, the coach often picks the child rather than the other way around. Many leagues, such as the AYSO, rate players and then place them in divisions 1 through 14, 1 being the most talented. Each coach either picks or is allotted a player from each category in order to make the teams as balanced as possible. You can, however, influence this decision. I have seen parents who specifically asked not to have their child be coached by certain people get their wish. This may hurt the coach's feelings, but it may also alert him or her that something he or she does needs correcting. Besides, if the choice is between getting the best for your child or protecting an adult's feelings, is there really a choice?

From the Doctor's Desk

If you have a bad coach, how do you go about working with him, airing constructive criticism, or even replacing him?

1. Assess if the problem is with the coach or with your expectations. Do this by asking your child if he's satisfied and asking other parents. For example, ask the child if he or she likes playing soccer, are they having fun, what are they learning, do they like the coach?
2. Approach the coach with your requests, preferably at a practice. Be positive, encourage his good work and effort. Then make a request for the changes you'd like to see.
3. If the above doesn't work, approach the league officials and ask them to intervene.

Complementary Coach

When selecting a coach think of your child's needs. Will this coach complement your child emotionally?

1. Does your child need a strong male or female role model?
2. If your child is assertive or aggressive, he or she would do best with a similar coach.
3. If your child is anxious or shy, often a female coach who is comforting and accepting would best suit him.

31

The Last Life Lesson

"There is always one more lesson to be learned"
—LAWRENCE ROBINSON

"Oh, no," I cried to myself as I turned my face away from Nicky, the goalie. I grimaced and gritted my teeth in disgust. Stephanie drove another shot right past her. The scoreboard seemed eighty feet high. High enough to be seen from miles away. High enough and bright enough to show the score: Black Bears 13, Good News Bears 0. At that moment the final whistle signaled the end of the game. Despite their valiant effort, my little players were losers. But it was not their fault. It was mine. As I looked up toward the sky, I thought how I really deserved this humiliation. But it was not over yet. Hank, two hundred pounds of redneck bully boy, stood over me, his wide grin revealing yellowed teeth. And he laughed, no, cackled. A deep, horrible, echoing cackle. An urgent, distant ring suddenly stirred me and, opening my eyes, I realized, thank the Lord, it was all a dream.

Why the Nightmare?

It all started one early morning in August, the first year I had my daughter on Hank's team. I was determined to change Hank, to show him the error of his ways, so I decided to coach alongside him. By the second year I realized that no words could deter him from his indomitable desire to win at any cost. So I moved on to coach another team, still harboring hopes that one day I'd be able to teach Hank a lesson in sportsmanship. No, it was not a calculated vendetta. It just seemed that way.

Hank always befriended the arrogant, "holier-than-thou" assistant coaches. You know, the clean-cut, clipboard-toting types. They never came right out and said they were better than you, but every condescending look somehow stirred something within me. I chose two women as my assistants: Judy and Hope. Judy summed it up perfectly when she compared Hank and his coaches to Darth Vader and his storm troopers.

At the outset of my inaugural season, the regional commissioner called a meeting of all the regional coaches to select players for the upcoming season. Each league at the time had its own way of selecting teams to make them fair. There were ten teams in our league and all the registered players were ranked in groups according to their ability. The ten coaches were then asked to select players on an alternating basis, one from each ability group.

As usual, I arrived late to the meeting, still worrying about the fifteen-year-old with a fever and a headache I had left in the emergency room waiting for test results. I grabbed two donuts, inhaled one instantly, and was just about to take a huge bite of the second when Harold, Hank's trim assistant coach, took a bite of his apple and shot me a disgusted look. I glanced at his washboard abdomen and then down at my own flabby midriff. My appetite promptly dissipated but I finished the donut.

Dick, our regional commissioner, called me over and said, "We're at the first round of the draw, Vince. You have first pick." Wow, what a stroke of luck, I thought, I get the pick of the best players. It was an easy choice. I looked at Judy and Sally and said, "Stephanie." I knew that would rile Hank. Stephanie was easily the best player in the league. I smiled and glanced over at Hank, only to see that familiar grin spread across his face. I looked back at Judy and Hope, puzzled. They didn't seem nearly as amused as I was. "Vince, you were late," Judy quietly whispered. "Hank insisted on putting your daughter in the group of top players. If you don't choose her, she won't be on your team." At that moment I felt like strangling Hank. My daughter Kaycee wasn't a bad player, but was not in the "best player" category.

Hank had wrangled to have Kaycee placed in the top category for a reason. I had no choice but to change my selection and take Kaycee. Hank had the second pick and, of course, snapped up Stephanie. I wasn't upset, mind you. I'm well beyond petty, childlike behavior to gain advantage at the price of decency and fair play.

By the third round, Hank and his henchmen had started protesting and cutting deals, all in the guise of friendly competition. Courage beckoned and I decided to confront him. Hank squarely faced me, ready for a showdown, our guns still holstered. Before Hank new what happened, I took the first shot. "Look, Hank," I said. "Why don't you take all my first picks and I'll take the players you don't want."

Hank grinned his yellow-toothed grin again. The other coaches smiled, amused that I had confronted Hank and his henchmen's manipulations before the season had even started. Hank, not surprisingly, accepted. Determined to have the last word, I fired another shot at Hank, before he could hit the ground. "And when my underdogs beat you and your hotshots, you'll finally understand what real coaching is all about." From the glint in his eyes I could tell he felt the sting of that remark.

The Season

Well, I certainly found out what coaching was all about pretty quickly. Hank's Black Bears routed us 7–0 the first time our teams met, mauled us 9–1 the second time, and 6–1 the third. The last Saturday of the season would be our final opportunity to exact some revenge over him and his under-twelve-year-old storm troopers.

During the season, we had plenty of opportunities to appreciate the old adage, "It's OK to lose, but don't lose the lesson." We were certainly losing, but I hoped the lesson had been learned and we could win this one. I know I've said that "losing is never fatal," but my sense of pride was on the line and I had to prove to the entire league that "good guys don't finish last."

The Saturday game was, of all things, scheduled at high noon. Hope and Judy were great. They ensured that all the parents attended a pregame party the night before. Really, it was a meeting for me to unite the parents before the big game in an effort to give our side every honorable advantage. Although the players were in the ten- to twelve-year-old range, their concentration could sometimes be interrupted by the confusion of an open game. So before the game, while the kids were warming up, I explained the "closed system" of play with the parents, the

need to have only the coaches giving directions, and the importance of cheering, especially when our team was down (something they were all accustomed to by now). Most important,
however, I stressed that every parent must maintain a positive
attitude and keep their cool, even when Hank and his henchmen ordered the Black Bears to play rough, aggressive, or dangerous soccer. If, or rather, *when* Hank bent the rules to his
advantage, we could show him that honesty and integrity is the
best policy and we hoped prove that the team that thinks they
can win, will win.

Under the Guise of Youth Soccer

The day had arrived. The teams assembled on the field, stretching, warming up. I gazed over at the Black Bears' bench to flash
Hank a smile. My players' parents, as I had asked, were mingling with the Black Bears' moms and dads. The kids also
smiled and showed deserved respect for the undefeated, power-
packed Black Bears who had run roughshod over us three times
that season already. But this was a new game, a new team. Since
our last defeat we had won four consecutive games. Not by
much, not against good teams, but they were victories nonetheless, meaningful and important to the players. Yes, we were the
Good News Bears, a name I chose to deliberately set ourselves
apart from Hank's team.

The sidelines were full. Not only with my team's parents,
but the coaches and parents of the previous game were still
hanging around. The regional commissioner had even invited
members of the board to this match. After all, it was only a kids'
game. But let me tell you, deep down, Judy, Hope, and every

parent on my team felt the same way. I think we had all had that same nightmare. If only we could just lose by a couple of goals, I thought. Please, God, just let us keep it close.

I looked over toward Hank again, who seemed unusually relaxed. I even thought I saw him smile. No, it had to be a snicker. As my players gathered around me, I started one of my well-known pep talks. I talked about the value of effort, honor, and perseverance, lacing my statements with asides about the character of team they faced. I was exorcising the nightmare of the previous night. "We must always respect the Black Bears," I told them. "Those girls are good, but remember how hard you've practiced. Now, how good are the Good News Bears?" I stopped for the answer and they yelled back in unison, "We're the best!"

I asked again, "How good are the Good News Bears?" and they yelled back, even louder, "We're the best!" Stirred by their enthusiasm, I urged them with my best Shakespearean battle cry. "No one can beat us when we play with honor, can they?"

But before they could answer, Kaycee's little brother, Michael, said, "They killed you the last three times, Dad." Oh, how could he say what I was sure was on every player and parent's mind, just when I was trying to make them forget it! I ignored him and quickly asked again. "There is no victory without honor," they answered. I asked them again and they shouted, "There is no victory without honor and respect!"

I continued, "Today you are already winners, because you are honorable. You are the best in my eyes and in your parents' eyes." We ended with our cheer. "Who are we?"

"The Good News Bears!" they repeated, louder each time.

The good news spread across the field from the first kickoff to the last tackle. Our team played with fire. The Black Bears played well, very well and, surprisingly for a team of Hank's,

there were no angry confrontations with the ref and no dangerous tackles. Hank even kept Stephanie, his number one striker,
out for all of the second half. Hope assured me it was because
she had turned her ankle but this didn't explain why he also left
out his second best player, Anne. She was known for her deadly
strikes from free kicks and penalties. She had not missed a shot
all year, Hank often bragged. She was his niece.

Though we were down 4–2 at the half, we pulled the game
back to a 5–5 tie by the final whistle. Now, it was time for kicks
from the penalty mark to decide the winner. I looked over at
Hank, his arms folded, and he looked right back at me, just like
the day of the draw four months ago. It was high noon.

Each team scored their first four penalty kicks. The game was
still tied. Then Jane stepped up for the Black Bears and sent her
shot sailing over the crossbar. If the Good News Bears could score
this last penalty, we would win 5–4. Everyone held his breath as
Linda limped over to the penalty mark: twelve yards from the goal
mouth. I could hardly watch. For all her enthusiasm and effort,
Linda was not a skillful player and I knew she was unlikely to even
manage to get the shot on target, let alone beat the Black Bears'
keeper. Linda awkwardly ran up to the ball and kicked it with all
her might. But she caught the ball with the outside of her foot,
sending it spinning off at a right angle, away from the goal. The
force and direction of the ball took everyone by surprise, however,
even the referee, who was standing to one side of the goal area.
Miraculously, the ball barely kissed the inside of the left goal post
and rebounded into the net, past the bemused Black Bears' goalie.

There was a moment's hesitation. No one was certain
whether the goal counted. Then the referee shrugged and whistled for the end of the game. The Good News Bears had won.
There was disbelief one moment, pandemonium the next. As I

watched the girls jump up and down everything seemed to slip into slow motion, the girls hanging in the air, elation frozen on their faces. Then reality slapped me on the back. I looked over at the Black Bears as they trudged dejectedly off the field. Why did Hank leave his best two players out for the entire second half? I asked myself. Why didn't his niece take a penalty kick? I was puzzled.

I couldn't see Hank anywhere. No doubt he had quickly left as he usually did. He had never shaken my hand after his previous three victories. I certainly didn't expect him to after a defeat. Then, as I turned away, I heard, "Good game, Vince," and a burly hand was shoved in front of me. Hank and his two henchmen stood there, smiling. I couldn't help asking him why he kept his best players out. He looked me straight in the eye and said, "You know, Vince, you rub off on people. You once told me there was more to learn from losing than from winning. I thought, gee, maybe I should see if he's right. Even if I lose, I'll really be winning anyway, right?" He shook my hand and said, "The best man won."

I looked him straight in the eye and shook my head. "The best man today, Hank, is you."

I gathered up the equipment and Kaycee and Michael ran over to me. "Gee, Dad, I never thought you could do it," said a wide-eyed Michael. "Even the regional commissioner said so, Dad." I laughed. Children are great, I thought.

We walked toward the parking lot as the sun dipped down behind the San Gabriel Mountains. I took a deep breath. Kaycee slipped her tiny hand in mine and said, "When does the next season start, Dad? I love soccer. Can I get a poster of Mia Hamm?" I thought, This is a dream. A dream of a season, a dream I'll always remember.

PART VII

WHAT IS THIS GAME CALLED SOCCER?

For most of the world's population, soccer—or football, *fútbol,
calcio*—is as important as the sun rising and setting each day. It
is something they've grown up with. For many in the United
States and Canada, however, soccer is a foreign, often misunderstood game. But it's the simplicity of soccer that holds the key
to its appeal. There are seventeen laws of soccer, compared to
232 for baseball. It's as simple as it is exciting. Soccer is not "un-
American" but is another great game like baseball and football
that brings families, towns, and countries together.

32

The Rules That Protect the Spirit of Soccer

For the many parents who are just discovering the game of soccer, what follows is a brief overview of the game, its rules, and some of the terminology involved. Remember, above all, soccer is just a game, a good game for children to have fun. All the rules and laws are second to the spirit of the game—namely, to ensure a safe and equal opportunity for each child so they can enjoy themselves and learn. The following is a summary of the rules as they are generally accepted. For youth soccer, some of the dimensions and the laws are altered by your youth soccer organization to enhance the safety and enjoyment of the game of soccer.

The Game

Part of the beauty of soccer is its simplicity. All you need is a field, a ball, two teams, and a referee. The field is approximately the size of a football field, maybe a little smaller for younger players, and the game is played in two halves of equal duration, although the American Youth Soccer Association (AYSO) advocates quarter breaks within each half to allow for player substitutions. The duration of each half is a maximum of forty-five minutes, less for younger players.

A team has a maximum of eleven players on the field at any one time, although games can be played with as few as five or seven on each team, which allows players more touches on the ball and enables them to learn ball control, passing, and shooting skills quicker.

Dimensions: The soccer field is rectangular, a little larger than a football field, 100 to 130 yards long and 50 to 100 yards wide, marked out as in the diagram. The halfway line (or midfield line) cuts the field exactly in two.

Boundaries: The field is bounded by two side or touchlines and two endlines or goal lines. The markings on the field are made by five-inch-wide white lines.

Goal Area: A goal is located in the center of each goal line, The goal area or six-yard box is the area immediately in front of each goal. Outside the goal area is the penalty area, the area in which the goalkeeper is allowed to use his hands.

Corner Arcs: At each corner of the field is a corner flag and a corner arc, in which the ball is placed for a corner kick.

The Center Circle: The center spot is in the exact center of the field—the place where kickoffs are taken at

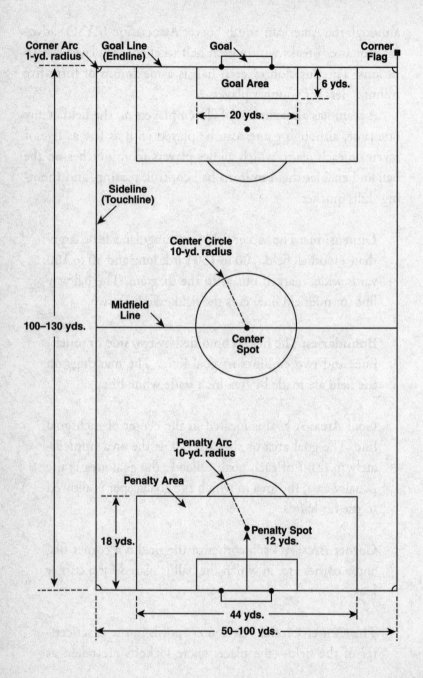

the beginning of each half and after each goal is scored. When a kickoff is taken, opposition players have to stand beyond the center circle, ten yards from the center spot.

The Penalty Area: The penalty spot is twelve yards from the goal line midway between each goalpost. When a penalty is taken all players except for the goalkeeper and the penalty kicker must be at least ten yards from the ball, i.e., outside the penalty area and beyond the penalty arc.

The Team

Soccer teams normally consist of players in four primary positions, as follows:

The Goalkeeper: Also known as the "keeper" or "goalie," who is responsible for guarding the team's goal and preventing the opposing team from scoring. The goalkeeper is the only player on the team allowed to use his hands, although only within the designated goal or "penalty" area.

Defenders: They are responsible for stopping the opposition from having a clear shot at goal. Defenders also work to gain possession of the ball and pass it to teammates to set up an attack.

Midfielders: As the name suggests, midfielders play between the defense and the forwards and are often the most active players on the field, linking defense and attack, and maintaining the flow of play.

Forwards: They have the primary responsibility of leading the attack on the opposition's goal and, as the front players (or "strikers"), often score the goals (although any player in soccer may score a goal, regardless of position). The forwards also assist the midfielders in shifting play from defense to offense.

The Skills

There are several basic skills in soccer that can be learned at any age and mastered by players who practice them regularly.

Passing: is kicking, pushing, or heading the ball to a teammate or to a space where a teammate can run on to the ball. A player may lightly tap the ball to a teammate several feet away or kick it strongly across or down the field. The ball can be played along the ground or through the air.

Dribbling: is performed by maintaining control of the ball with the feet and weaving in and out of opposing players.

Controlling: is checking the ball from a pass by stopping or "trapping" it with the inside of the foot or allowing it to bounce off the chest, head, or thigh at an angle that deflects it to the ground to be controlled by the feet.

Heading: is used to stop or pass a ball that's too high to kick or control with your chest. It's also used effectively to score goals and defend high balls.

Tackling: is a way of gaining possession of the ball. A player strikes hard for the ball, meeting it determinedly with the inside of his or her foot and forcing it out of the opponent's possession.

Shooting: A player gets all his weight behind the shot and follows through with the striking foot. To keep the ball low, he makes sure the knee of the striking leg is over the ball at the moment of impact.

Goalkeepers' Skills

Making a save: A goalie should try to get her body behind the shot, so that if the ball slips through her hands, her body acts as a second barrier to prevent it going into the net for a goal.

Diving: Dives are made side-toward-the-ground, allowing the goalkeeper to get his or her body behind the ball and watch the flight of the ball as it travels toward the goal.

Punching the ball: If the goalie is under great pressure from attacking players, he or she will sometimes punch a high ball away, preferably using both fists, to send the ball as far away from the goal as possible.

The Officials

There are usually three game officials: one referee, who has ultimate authority over the game, and two assistant referees, who signal to the referee when the ball has gone out of play and which team has possession. Sometimes a fourth official is used on the touchline to supervise substitutions and any additional time to be added to the game.

The Laws of the Game

Generally, the laws of soccer require that referees stop the game when something has happened that is unfair or unsafe.

The object: The object of soccer is, of course, for players to get the ball into their opponent's goal using any part of their body except their arms and hands.

The whole of the ball: The whole ball must be over the goal line between the goal posts for a goal to be scored; similarly, the whole ball must cross the sideline or touchline to be out of play.

Kickoff: A kickoff is taken from the center circle at the beginning of the game, at the beginning of the second half, and after each goal.

Throw-in: When the ball has completely crossed the sidelines—or touchlines—a throw-in is awarded against the team that last touched the ball. The throw-in is

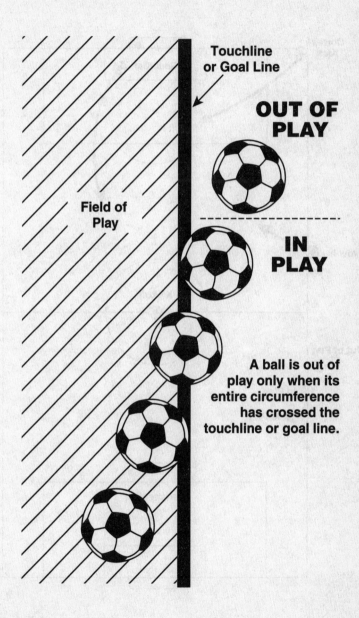

Touchline
or Goal Line

OUT OF
PLAY

Field of
Play

IN
PLAY

A ball is out of
play only when its
entire circumference
has crossed the
touchline or goal line.

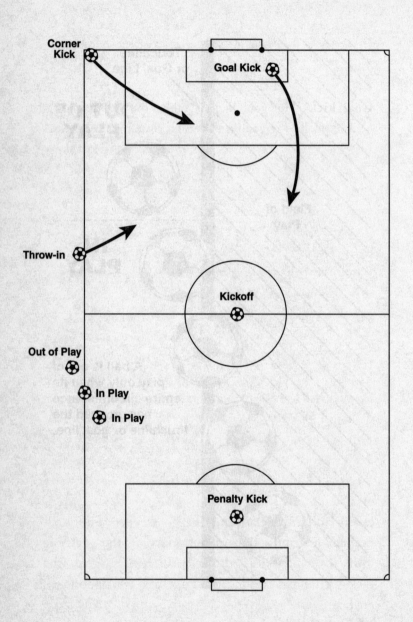

taken from where the ball left the field and must be thrown with two hands from behind and over the head, while both feet are on the ground on or behind the touchline.

Goal kick: The goal kick is taken by the defending team (usually the goalkeeper) each time the ball crosses the goal line and was last touched by an attacking player. The ball may be placed anywhere in the goal area and is not considered back in play until it has been kicked out of the penalty area.

Corner kick: The corner kick is taken by the attacking team each time the ball is knocked out by the defense over its own goal line. The ball is placed within the three-foot arc in the corner of the field (nearest to where the ball went out of play) and kicked into play by the attacking team.

Penalty kick: The penalty kick is awarded when a defending player commits a serious foul within his own penalty area. The penalty kick is taken by a player from the offended team from a spot twelve yards from the goal. All players must remain outside the penalty area, ten yards from the ball, until the kick is taken, except for the kicker and the goalkeeper. The goalkeeper's feet must remain stationary on the goal line until the ball is kicked. At the referee's signal, the kicker attempts to kick the ball into the opponent's goal and the goalkeeper tries to stop the ball from crossing the goal line.

Fouls and Misconduct

There are three kinds of misconduct:

Minor infringements resulting in a free kick, actions resulting in a caution (a yellow card) from the referees, and actions resulting in a player being sent off or ejected from the field (a red card). A second yellow card automatically results in a red card and ejection from the game.

> **Offside**: A player is offside if she is ahead of the ball in the opponent's half of the field unless two opponents are between them and the opponent's goal line at the moment at which the ball is played (rather than when it is received).
>
> Offsides can be ignored by the referees if the player in an offside position is not involved in active play or interfering with play, interfering with an opponent, or gaining an advantage by being in that position. There can be no offside directly from a corner, a throw-in, or if in your own half of the field.

Fouls that result in a direct free kick, from which a goal may be directly scored against the opponents, are as follows:

- Kicking or attempting to kick an opponent, without playing the ball.
- Striking or attempting to strike an opponent.
- Pushing, charging, tripping, holding, jumping on, or impeding an opponent.
- When tackling an opponent, making contact with the opponent before or instead of the ball.

OFFSIDE

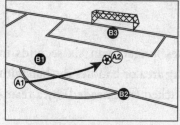

Only the Goalkeeper B3 is between Attacker A2 and the goal.

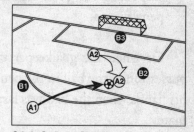

Only the Goalkeeper B3 was between Attacker A2 and the goal when the ball left A1's foot.

ONSIDE

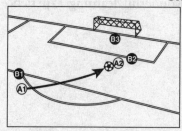

Two Defenders, B2 and Goalkeeper B3, are between Attacker A2 and the goal.

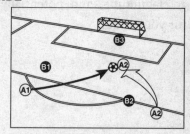

Defender B1 and Goalkeeper B3 were between A2 and the goal when the ball left A1's foot.

- Handling the ball deliberately.
- Unsportsmanlike behavior.

An indirect free kick, which requires at least one additional player of either team to touch the ball before a goal can be scored, is awarded for:

Dangerous play: such as high kicking near another player's head or trying to play a ball held by a goal-keeper.

Obstruction: getting between an opponent and the ball when not playing the ball.

Impeding the goalkeeper: excessive contact within the penalty area.

Or when the goalkeeper takes longer than six seconds in possession of the ball in the penalty area or handles the ball with his hands when the ball was last kicked (not headed) by a teammate.

And that's all there is to it. Just add excitement, a roaring crowd, and the drama of a close game and you have a fun, character-building, and potentially wonderful learning experience for your child.

Glossary of Soccer Terms

ADVANTAGE RULE: a clause in the rules that permits the referee to refrain from stopping the play for a foul if the team that was fouled already has possession of the ball and is in a good attacking position.

ASSIST: one player passes to another and he or she scores.

ATTACKER: a forward or striker.

ATTACKING TEAM: the team that has possession of the ball.

AYSO: American Youth Soccer Organization.

BACK: a defender.

BEAT: to get the ball past an opponent by dribbling, passing, or shooting.

BEHIND THE DEFENDER: the area between a defender and his goal.

BREAK: when a team quickly advances the ball down the field before the opposition has a chance to retreat.

CAUTION: see "yellow card."

CENTER: a cross or pass from a player located near the sideline toward the middle of the field; used to get the ball closer to the front of the goal.

CENTRAL DEFENDER: a player who plays in the middle of defense, directly in front of his goalkeeper.

292 ⚽ **Glossary of Soccer Terms**

CLEAR: to kick the ball away from the area near one's goal.

CLEATS: the metal, plastic, or rubber "studs" in the bottom of a soccer boot used to provide traction; term also used to refer to the boots themselves.

CLUB: a team that plays in a league.

COUNTERATTACK: an attack launched by a defending team soon after it regains possession of the ball.

CREATING SPACE: when a player from the attacking team moves away from the ball in order to draw defenders away from his teammate with the ball carrier and so give him space.

CROSS: see "center."

DANGEROUS PLAY: when a player uses his feet to kick a head-height ball when an opposing player is also challenging for the ball. For example, any attempt to play what the referee considers dangerous to that player or others.

DEFENDERS: the backs: fullbacks, center backs, stopper, sweeper.

DEFENDING TEAM: the team that does not have possession of the ball.

DEFLECTION: the ricochet of a ball after it hits a player, post, or referee.

DIVING HEADER: a ball struck by the head of a diving player.

DRAW: a game that ends with a tied score.

DROP BALL: a way of restarting the game; the referee drops the ball between two players facing each other.

DROP KICK: when a goalie kicks the ball from his penalty area by dropping it from his hands and kicking it before it hits the ground.

ENDLINE: see "goal line."

FAKE OR FEINT: a "dummy" move meant to deceive an opposing player; used by a ball carrier to make a defender think the ball carrier is going to dribble, pass, or shoot in a certain direction when he is not.

FAR POST: the goalpost furthest from the ball.

FOOTBALL: name for soccer in most countries except the United States.

FORMATION: the arrangement of players on the field; for example, in eleven-a-side soccer, a "4–4–2 formation" means a team is playing with one goalkeeper, four defenders, four midfielders, and two forwards (the goalkeeper is not listed—every formation plays with just one goalkeeper).

FORWARDS: the attackers, strikers, wingers on the team who are responsible for most of the scoring.

FOUL: a violation of the rules for which an official assesses a free kick or penalty.

FULLBACKS: defenders who play near the touchlines—a left back and a right back respectively.

GOAL KICK: a way of restarting the game when the ball crossed the goal line last touched by an attacking player; the ball is kicked from anywhere inside the goal area.

GOAL LINE: the endline.

GOALMOUTH: the front opening to each goal.

HALFBACK: another (outdated) term for a midfielder.

HALFTIME: the intermission between the two periods or halves of a game.

HAND BALL: a foul where a player other than the goalie touches the ball with his hand or arm.

HAT TRICK: three goals scored in a game by a single player.

IN PLAY: when a ball is within the boundaries of the field and play has not been stopped by the referee.

INJURY TIME: time added on to the end of any half due to player injuries, substitutions, or intentional delays by a team.

LINESMEN: the assistant referees who patrol the touchlines.

LOFT OR LOB: a high-arcing kick.

MARKING: guarding a player to prevent him from passing or receiving the ball.

MATCH: a soccer game.

MIDFIELD: the region of the field near the center line; the area controlled by the midfielders.

MIDFIELDERS: the players who link together the offensive and defensive functions of a team; they play between the forwards and the defenders.

NEAR POST: the goalpost closest to the ball.

NET: the mesh draped over the frame of the goal to catch the ball when a goal is scored.

OBSTRUCTION: when a defensive player uses his body to prevent an offensive player from playing the ball.

OFFENSIVE PLAYER: see "attacker."

OFFENSIVE TEAM: see "attacking team."

OFFICIALS: the referee and two or three assistants who officiate a game of soccer.

OFFSIDE: a violation called when a player in an offside position receives a pass or interferes with play.

OFFSIDE POSITION: an attacking player positioned so that fewer than two opposing defensive players (usually the goalie and one other defender) are between him and the goal he is attacking when he receives the ball.

ONSIDE: the opposite of offside.

OPEN: a player who does not have anyone marking him.

OUT OF BOUNDS: when a ball is outside the boundaries of the field.

OUT OF PLAY: see "out of bounds."

OVERTIME: or "extra time" is the periods played after regulation when the game ends tied.

PENALTY: short for penalty kick; also, a punishment given by the referee for a violation of the rules within the penalty area.

PENALTY KICK: a kick taken from the penalty spot by a player against the opposing goalie.

PITCH: a British term for soccer field.

PLAY ON: a term used by referees to indicate that the advantage rule has been applied and no stoppage is to be called.

POSSESSION: control of the ball.

POST: goalpost.

RED CARD: a card that a referee holds up to signal a player's removal from the game.

REFEREE: the chief official.

REGULAR SEASON: the schedule of games played before a playoff is held.

SAVE: the act of a goalkeeper in blocking or stopping a shot on goal.

SCORE: to put the ball into the net for a goal; the tally of goals during a game.

SCORERS: players who score goals.

SCREENING: see "shielding."

SET PLAY: a planned play from a "dead-ball situation" such as a corner kick or free kick.

SHIELDING: a way for the player in possession of the ball to protect it from a defender by keeping his body between the ball and the defender.

SHIN GUARDS: shin pads that protect the front of a player's legs.

SHOOTING: when a player kicks the ball at the opponent's net in an attempt to score a goal.

SHORT-SIDED OR SMALL-SIDED GAME: a game played with fewer than eleven players per side.

SHOT: a ball kicked or headed at the opponent's net in an attempt to score a goal.

SHUTOUT: preventing the opposition from scoring any goals in a game.

SIDELINE OR TOUCHLINE: the line that runs along the length of the field on each side.

SLIDING TACKLE: sliding on the ground feet-first to make a tackle on an opposing player who has possession of the ball.

SQUARE PASS: a pass made by one player to a teammate alongside him or her.

STOPPER: the defender that marks the opposition's best scorer with the aim of "stopping" him from scoring.

STRIKER: a team's best-scoring center forward.

SUBSTITUTION: replacement of one player on the field with another player not on the field.

SWEEPER: the defender that plays closest to his own goal behind the rest of the defenders; a team's last line of defense in front of the goal-keeper.

TOUCHLINE: see "sideline."

TRAP: when a player uses his body to slow down and control a moving ball, using his chest, thighs, head, or feet.

USYSA: United States Youth Soccer Association.

VOLLEY: a ball kicked by a player before it hits the ground.

WALL: a line of defending players standing together to protect their goal against a close free kick.

WINGS: the areas of the field closest to the touchlines.

WINGERS: the attacking players who play along the wings with the aim of crossing the ball in to the forwards.

WORLD CUP: the international soccer competition held by FIFA (Fédération Internationale de Football Association) every four years between the top national teams in the world.

YELLOW CARD: a card that a referee holds up to warn a player for dangerous or unsportsmanlike behavior; also called a caution; two yellow cards in one game earns a player an automatic red card, signaling his removal from the game.

Index

About the Author

Vincent Fortanasce, M.D., is a neurologist, psychiatrist, bio-ethicist, Little League Hall of Famer, former Olympic athlete, and devoted soccer dad. He currently practices neurology at Los Angeles County Hospital and is also the author of *Life Lessons from Little League.*

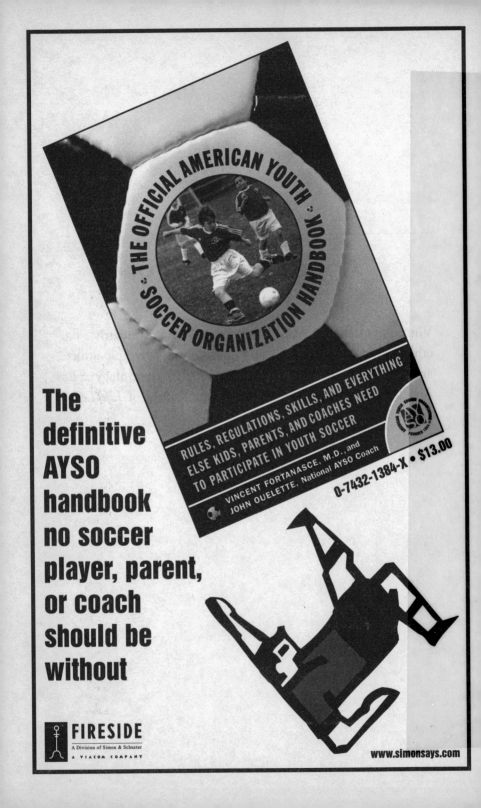